Readers Respond
I Made It Through

"*I Made it Through* is such *a powerful testimonial* of God's goodness and faithfulness to you especially. We really thank God for your life. I started and almost finished reading the book on my flight to Lagos a few days ago. What a great inspiration and encouragement it is and will be to multitudes. Well done . . . Praise God indeed! I wish you and your family all the blessings of this season and a happy, prosperous and fruitful new year ahead in Jesus' name. We celebrate you and God bless you!"

—PASTOR LEKE SANUSI,
RCCG VICTORY HOUSE, LONDON, UK

"Absolutely Inspiring-Must Read! I *absolutely loved this book* and I recommend everyone read it. This book is a beautiful representation of God working in a strong woman's life today in a very real way. Bukky tells her life testimony in a clever and truthful fashion including not just the blessings she has experienced but also the challenges anyone walking on God's path will experience. Throughout the book, you can see her passion and the

deference she has towards Jesus and the great blessings God has worked in her life as a result. The Bible verses throughout the book made me stop and think about my own path and were very valuable, but my favorite portion of the book was the journal entries at the very end. Her testimony of giving up everything to her faith in God is simply inspiring and encourages me to ask questions and take my own steps into a life of faith."

—GRETA D., USA

"Dear Sister Bukky, I am in Addis and have read your book during the flight. What *a remarkable story* of faith, courage, determination. You remind me of Moses who left Egypt and a life of ease. You left London and a financial career in pursuit of the will of God and stepped out in faith with nothing under you but the word of God. You are a woman of faith and God is pleased when we walk by faith . . . . Gods grace and glory is on you and surrounds you. Lots of blessings! Your fellow-servant in Christ."

—EKKEHARD HORNBURG, GERMANY

"Wow I read your book on the plane. I was just thanking God for your life. Your style of writing is *so engaging* and your memory so sharp. Amazing all the ups and downs, divine appointments and your 'forceful faith' let downs, disappointments. Hmmmm one could never have guessed that you went through all that struggle. Still can't get over all the divine encounters and people showing unusual favor and 'open doors.' I celebrate you! You really made it through and you're standing strong. Alleluiaaaaaaa."

—BIBI BUNMI APAMPA, BEST SELLING AUTHOR, TOP MOTIVATIONAL SPEAKER & BUSINESS CONSULTANT, UK

"One of your books, *I Made It Through* was donated to the Isolation Centre I was during Covid 19 in Nigeria and I had a chance to read it because I worked as a support staff there. It was really *great and interesting to read!* I hope to read it again."

—CHARLES LAWAL. NIGERIA, AFRICA

"In eighteen intriguing chapters, Agboola examines different themes. In the early chapters, the reader is given *a firsthand glimpse* of the responsibilities placed on the firstborn in Agboola's culture. After arriving in the UK, Agboola is left to care for her siblings after the untimely death of her father. In chapter six, when she breaks down at the graduation ceremony of her younger brother, we see how those we look up to and regard as unbreakable are human, too. Agboola's memoir explores the hardships that firstborn children face. She also touches on how parents often seem to forget that they, too, are in need of care.

When one thinks of wealth one often thinks in material terms. Agboola's memoir, however, views it in different forms. The first is the priceless nature of good health. This is examined through the death of both her parents and the miraculous healing of her daughter's fracture. Agboola reminds the reader that although money is important for survival, one must first be alive. She also examines wealth in terms of relationships. Although the modern world encourages distant relationships via technology, it has become increasingly difficult to find true meaning in love and kinship. In all the tribulations she and her family face, Agboola finds strength in God, mostly through the meaningful human relationships she builds over time.

Through the Faith Dairy, which forms the memoir's epilogue, the author examines the truth behind the popular belief that those who give cheerfully receive a tenfold return. In what seem to be blind acts of charity, she sows seeds of wealth into various individuals and organisations, even when her own family is in dire need. The memoir challenges readers to test their beliefs and make others smile. Agboola and her family give wholeheartedly because they know that others are in greater need and not because they want to be praised or admired.

While some believe that we create our own destinies, others believe that our destinies are already set in stone and that we can do no more than access them by making the right choices. In this memoir, destiny repeatedly beckons to the author. This memoir also examines the courage one needs to take risks in the name of following what one believes to be one's destiny or perhaps the voice of God. In her own case, Agboola attempts to delay her destiny but this ultimately proves futile. In comparison to the biblical story of God's directive to Abraham to leave his father's land for a new, unknown land, Agboola's family is also tested by destiny and, perhaps, God to leave good in order to find better.

Although mainly directed at Christians, Agboola's memoir can teach people of other faiths . . . . In every situation she passes through, the author never forgets God. She challenges the reader to put their own faith to work when they find themselves in dire straits. In the last chapter, she promises that faith in tandem with good works will always be fruitful.

Through her various tribulations—the pain of both parents dying in terrible ways, the risk of leaving everything she knew behind for an unknown land, a decade of territorial disputes and bouts of doubt—the author finds strength in the scriptures. In this *uplifting memoir*, she gives the reader hope that every tribulation can be overcome."

—WAWA BOOK REVIEW BY TIMI ODUESO NIGERIA. AFRICA

"An encouraging and fast read! A glimpse into seeing what faith would look like in a modern day life. Very inspiring!"

—Danielle E., USA

I
Made
It Through

Making Successful
Transitions by Trusting in God

Bukky Agboola

CHORDS OF LOVE LLC

Author's contact information
Websites: www.bukkymusic.com

Book design by DesignforBooks.com

Printed in the United States of America.

Contents

Foreword · vii

Dedication and Preface · xi

Chapter One
Growing Up Grateful · 1

Chapter Two
First God Encounters · 9

Chapter Three
College Days · 15

Chapter Four
Things Fall Apart · 19

Chapter Five
God's Faithfulness · 27

Chapter Six
Canon by Pachelbel · 33

Chapter Seven

Hope Renewed · 41

Chapter Eight

God's Destiny Finds You · 49

Chapter Nine

The Prophetic Unlocks Destiny · 59

Chapter Ten

Honoring God's Servants · 71

Chapter Eleven

1995, a Pivotal Year · 77

Chapter Twelve

1995, God's Just Getting Started · 85

Chapter Thirteen

Audacious Faith Move to America · 91

Chapter Fourteen

Arriving in a Strange Land · 105

Chapter Fifteen

Trouble · 113

Chapter Sixteen
Devastating News · 121

Chapter Seventeen
God's Early Preparation · 129

Chapter Eighteen
Faith Diary · 133

FOREWORD

In the Old Testament, we find the story of Ruth, a hopeless young Gentile widow who never would have inherited God's blessings if she had stayed in the forsaken land of Moab. She had to leave her home and travel to Bethlehem with her mother-in-law, Naomi. Once Ruth was repositioned, she discovered God's salvation and favor—and she ended up in the lineage of the Messiah.

The Bible is full of stories of people who had to move from one place to another to align with God's plans. Abram and Sarai left their relatives in Ur; Moses had to lead the Hebrews out of Egypt; Nehemiah had to travel from Persia to Jerusalem. In the New Testament, Peter had to go to Cornelius' house in Caesarea; Paul had to sail to Rome; and God had to scatter the disciples (see Acts 8:1) so they would fulfill the Great Commission.

None of these transitions was easy. We prefer the comfort of the familiar and the security of a steady paycheck. But faith is a journey, and it often leads us to places we would never choose on our own.

This is why I appreciate this memoir by Bukky Agboola. She had to journey from her native Nigeria to a foreign land to discover her spiritual calling.

As I have pondered Bukky's message, I've found myself asking questions about my own alignment. Am I in the right place to receive from God? Is He calling me to shift in any way—either geographically or in my relationships? Many respected prophetic voices have been talking recently about alignment because it is a crucial issue for God's people.

When the Lord is getting ready to do a new thing, He repositions us. God wants us in the right place at the right time. Are you in proper alignment? Here are a few questions to ponder as you read Bukky's story:

1. **Are you part of a faith community?** I meet many Christians today who tell me they have stopped attending a local church, either because they were wounded by a pastor or because they feel that church is irrelevant to them. I don't doubt that the wounds are real. But to pull away from the church is to cut yourself off from the fullness of His blessing. As imperfect as the church is, it is still His plan. God's anointing has never rested on lone rangers who are motivated by independent spirits.

   Corrie ten Boom once wrote: "When a Christian shuns fellowship with other Christians, the devil smiles." Please don't let bitterness or disillusionment give Satan an advantage in your life.

2. **Do you have mentors?** Oftentimes the reason we are not where we need to be spiritually is that we are

not connected to the people who can help us reach our full potential. Ruth needed Naomi to reach her destiny, Elisha needed Elijah, and Timothy needed Paul. Genuine discipleship is not about a person controlling you—it is about having an older, more experienced Christian in your life to provide loving encouragement and wise counsel. Don't try to do life alone. God wants to place special people in your path to propel you forward.

3. **Are you in any unhealthy relationships?** Abraham had to separate from Lot, and David had to leave Saul's house. Sometimes people can hinder our fruitfulness in ministry, especially if they refuse to submit to God's agenda. Don't be unequally yoked. Lot's wife died because her relationships in Sodom held a vise grip on her soul, preventing her from relocating into the safety of God's will. Now is the time to escape from toxic people who are thwarting you.

4. **Are you in the center of God's will?** People constantly ask me how they can discern the will of God for their lives. I don't believe there is a cookie-cutter formula, but it is not difficult to know God's will if we (1) read the Bible consistently, (2) pray fervently, (3) develop a submissive will, and (4) expect to hear His voice. The key to hearing God lies in your willingness to obey.

God still speaks today. Just as He told Abram to leave his father's country and go "to the land which I will show you" (Genesis 12:1, *New American Standard Bible*), He can give you clear directions. If you desire to know His plans for you, He will reveal them. He does not dangle carrots in front of us, nor does He play emotional games to keep us in the dark. He beckons us to align with His will, and His greatest blessings await us when we make the faith journey.

I believe your faith will be strengthened as you read Bukky's story. Let faith arise as you continue your own journey with Christ.

J. Lee Grady, Author, *10 Lies the Church Tells Women*, and *10 Lies Men Believe*
Director, The Mordecai Project
themordecaiproject.org

DEDICATION AND PREFACE

This memoir is dedicated to the Lord Jesus Christ as a testament to His faithful love. I am very sensitive to how much people hurt in our world. This book is birthed out of some of the hardest years for my family. The "lows" have, for me, been most fruitful. From the blessing of God's call on my life to enjoying the friendship of two of gospel music's most legendary names and the success of my family members in Nigeria and the United Kingdom, it may appear that we have experienced only the best in life. We have, however, come through many difficult years. Reading about that may come as a surprise to some people. More than two decades later, I am deeply grateful and humbled to have been able to impart God's amazing grace to inspire and empower others, and to have an amazing life story to share!

> No, dear brothers and sisters, I have not achieved it, but I focus on this one thing: Forgetting the past and looking forward to what lies ahead, I press on to reach the end of the race and receive the heavenly prize for which God, through Christ Jesus, is calling us. (Philippians 3:13–14, *Holy Bible, New Living Translation*)

Be blessed.
Bukky

Chapter One

GROWING UP GRATEFUL

It was the late 1980s, and I was sitting in the back of a black cab when, just after entering the first set of Buckingham palace gates, all traffic ground to a halt. *What's going on?* I thought. *I don't want to be late! Getting to work today will be a rush job.* I was only a short distance from home when all traffic suddenly stopped. Knowing that we were a stone's throw away from a world-renowned royal residence, I wondered what on Earth was serious enough to cause a major traffic disruption during the morning rush hour. *Yup, that's life for you,* I thought, *this sort of thing only happens on days when you are in a hurry and can least afford to waste time.* Then, as I was looking through the taxi windows, a heartwarming scene unfolded before me that still makes me smile all these years later.

An anxious-looking mother duck with a beautiful set of newly hatched golden ducklings was about to cross the street. They were headed toward the huge Queen Victoria Memorial roundabout in front of the palace. To prevent the duck and her babies from being crushed by busy morning commuters, a policeman had stopped all oncoming vehicles. The worried mother duck looked very frightened by all the noise from the hustle and bustle of commuters trying to reach their various destinations. The policeman proceeded to very carefully and gently guide her and her babies safely across the street. I'm sure that there were many varying reactions, but I and others around me said a collective "Aww." This scene was so quintessentially London—my current city of refuge—modern, yet quaint.

My new life here always made me feel safe and cozy, just like a cup of tea. That particular day had begun with a quick dash through the front doors to flag a taxicab on the corner of St. George's Drive and Victoria Street. The driver took the quick route through the first set of Buckingham Palace gates, down the mall, out through the second gates to Trafalgar Square, and on to my company's offices at the west end of Denmark Street. This wasn't the usual daily routine, but on days when I'm tired or almost late, this was the quickest and easiest way to work. The usual route would be a brisk walk to Pimlico or the Victoria underground station, a quick ride with the usual morning throng of commuters to Tottenham Court Road, and then a few minutes' walk to work.

～⁂～

I was the oldest of four children born to Nigerian parents, Elder Olu and Rev. Mrs. Sola Olarewaju. London was my second home. I had spent a large portion of my childhood and teenage years growing up in Ibadan, Oyo State, Nigeria. They were fun-filled days, with the usual ups and downs of daily life. We were two girls, then quickly followed by two boys. My siblings were my favorite playmates. The years I spent growing up in Nigeria were hectic and busy. The family usually began and ended each day with daily devotions but, as a young child, I would on many occasions lay in bed, hoping in my lazy, childish mind that my parents would be too tired to conduct this daily ritual.

⌒✐⌒

I wish they'd forget and fall asleep, so I could sleep longer, I would think, but, no, they never missed a day and had purchased a lovely little bell to tinkle us a reminder, calling us all to gather in our living room for devotions. One of our parents would start a hymn, and the morning scripture would always be Psalm 23, while the evening's was Psalm 121. I grew to know them both by heart. The day's chores begin with feeding our four dogs (mine was named Brownie because his coat was mostly a beautiful brown with a dab of white) and then getting dropped off at school. Our dad dropped us off and picked us up from school before his work day started. Rain or shine, tired or not, he was never late—always on time. Before school was out, the fond memory of the comforting sight of my father's parked car waiting, having arrived early to pick us up from school, is etched in my memory bank. He would quickly drop us off at home before continuing on with his work day. Now a parent myself, I honestly don't know how he managed that so faithfully. Always in our hearts, thanks Dad!

Homework and reading my favorite storybooks were the usual fare on weeknights. On the weekends, I eagerly waited for my dad to buy me the latest copies of the popular girl's comics and annuals imported from England. With much excitement, I would flip through the pages of the latest Jinty, Tammy, Bunty, and other favorites and soak in the newest escapades of my best-loved heroines. My dad was the one who gave me most of the annuals on special occasions like birthdays and Christmas, and, oh, what joy that would bring. They were packed with stories, and I wouldn't have to wait until the next edition for my happy endings.

We were content enough to go along with our weekly routines. Attending church on Sundays was also routine. Although my parents were Anglicans by denomination, they sent their children to Sunday school at the nearby Baptist Church near Loyola College in Ibadan, where Reverend Lawoyin presided as pastor. Playing hop-scotch with the next-door neighbor's children, giggling about silly stuff, worrying about my grades, and sneaking sips from the bottles of orange Fanta that Mom kept for our guests were all part of the fun times. Being the oldest child and a female, my parents assigned me the role of junior mom and leader of the pack. They instilled in me a very deep sense of responsibility for the care of the family whenever they were unavailable. Our African culture's very strong emphasis on respecting the oldest among us also greatly strengthened this pecking order.

Nursery and elementary school were at the Oritamefa Baptist Nursery and Primary school in Ibadan. Both our parents were educators by profession and were very strict disciplinarians. They also had cultivated in me a great love for reading, and I always enjoyed a big head start in all my subjects before getting into the classroom. Weekdays at the elementary school began with lining up for the morning assembly. We would sing songs of praise to God from small hymnals (I didn't notice at the time, but this must have been part of where my love of singing began. More about that later.) Then we would listen to a few words of inspiration for our little hearts from our headmistress, Mrs. Adeniyi, before we marched to our various classrooms.

Singing from my *Songs of Praise* hymnal and excelling at reading my Janet and John books were the greatest joys of my childish heart during this period. Happily, I completed elementary school, and after a rigorous test and interview process, I gained admission into the then private and very prestigious Catholic, all-girls high school, St. Teresa's College, in Ibadan. Learning came easily to me, with both my parents being there to help. My love for reading remained as we learned modern

African literature, including the works of African authors such as Chinua Achebe's *Things Fall Apart* and Camara Laye's *The African Child*, and we still covered classic literature from Shakespeare and so forth. New favorite teachers, debate teams, yearly bazaars, the tuck shop—where we rushed to buy snacks at lunchtime—and many other activities made my high school years fly by quickly and happily.

My fondest high-school memories include singing in music class for Miss Penny, learning to speak and sing in French in Sister Eileen's French class, being in Miss Bola's English class, and listening to the gentle, reassuring voice of our high school principal Sister Agnes Hassan at morning assembly. She was unusually beautiful, and even her required nun's attire and no-makeup face were unable to diminish her loveliness. Elegant yet most simple and soft-spoken, her authority was firm and unchallenged; she was one of my first heroines. This graceful nun became the epitome of womanhood that I still aspire to be today. Alas, I have a very long way to go!

The Nigerian social life consisted mostly of visits with and from my many aunties, uncles, and family friends for birthday, wedding, and other celebrations. My memories of Christmas time were the most special. Bringing home a real Christmas tree, our mother would take the time to create and decorate it with beautiful handmade ornaments. She also sewed all four of us brand-new outfits to celebrate this most wonderful time of the year. New Year's Eves at the home of my maternal grandmother, Victoria Badejoko, would follow. During these yearly visits, the sounds of her heartfelt morning prayers as she offered to God her daily morning devotions left another indelible print on my young heart. My siblings, cousins, and other young relatives would all eagerly look forward to the evening watchnight service on December 31 at our grandma's church, St. Peter's Cathedral, in Ibadan to usher in the New Year. It was the only time we were allowed to go out so late at night. We all eagerly and excitedly looked forward to it. I can still hear the beautiful sound of the large piping cathedral organ filling the huge building and coming through the walls as we all sang:

O God, our help in ages past, our hope for years to come, our shelter from the stormy blast, and our eternal home.

Under the shadow of thy throne, still may we dwell secure; sufficient is thine arm alone, and our defense is sure.

Before the hills in order stood, or earth received her frame, from everlasting, thou art God, to endless years the same.

A thousand Ages, in thy sight, are like an evening gone; short as the watch that ends the night, before the rising sun.

Time, like an ever-rolling stream, bears all who breathe away; they fly forgotten, as a dream dies at the opening day.

O God, our help in ages past, our hope for years to come; be thou our guide while life shall last, and our eternal home.

(Isaac Watts, "O God, Our Help in Ages Past," 1708)

This old wonderful hymn would conclude the service and open up the New Year. We would then go back home to joyfully begin the year!

Chapter Two

FIRST GOD ENCOUNTERS

As a child, during visits to our grandparents' house for the holidays, I loved attending a small local church near their home. Whenever there was a lull in the boisterous end-of-year festivities at home, I would find myself drawn to join in the happy singing and fervent prayer services of the little church next door. This happened every year, and I especially enjoyed and looked forward to these intimate worship times before the major New Year's Eve watchnight event at the much larger St. Peter's Cathedral. At the young age of twelve, during my high school years, I had an experience with God that would be my "born-again" experience.

Although our parents identified religiously as Christians, prayed daily with us at home, and made their children attend Sunday school regularly, our family did not yet know what it meant to be born again or be believers in and disciples of the Lord Jesus Christ (Christians). My parents were members of the same Anglican Church as my grandmother, St. Peter's Cathedral in Ibadan, and were members of the Church's Christ band. I can still remember my parents having many fun evenings socializing with the other members of their church group in our home, as they all rotated gathering at one another's homes. Attending church, but not regularly, as a religious, social, and morally responsible act was what our Christianity at the time mainly consisted of.

Believing we were already children of God, our hearts had not yet been penetrated with, or transformed by, the knowledge of our need for repentance from our sins and belief in the sacrifice of Jesus Christ, God's son, that brings us forgiveness, grace, and eternal life in heaven with God. I was soon to be divinely led to this most important and very first of faith principles: That true faith in God begins with being born again.

But as many as received Him, to them He gave the right to become children of God, even to those who believe in His name. (John 1:12, NASB)

Jesus answered and said to him, "Truly, truly, I say to you, unless one is born again he cannot see the kingdom of God." (John 3:3, NIV)

For God so loved the world that he gave his one and only Son, that whoever believes in him shall not perish but have eternal life. (John 3:16, NIV)

A family member had one day invited me to a large church retreat hosted by a Christian fellowship where for the first time I heard new worship songs that were quite different from our usual denominational church hymns. These were followed by the Holy Spirit-empowered gospel message. I was also taken to a church rally, which included a play. It was held on a Friday or Saturday night on the grounds of the Oritamefa Baptist Church congregational hall. The church was familiar to me as it was right next to my old elementary school, which had been founded by that denomination. The service's being held inside was, however, totally unfamiliar! There was joyful singing and clapping, and a play was dramatized to share the gospel. At the end of the play, a young man sang a special song, which included the lyrics,

> I'm gonna rise so high, now when the spirit spreads its wings across the sky
> The Risen One is comin' to take me away,
> I'm gonna live forever in His kingdom someday.[1]

Many years later in 2018, during a visit to the beautiful island of Jamaica, I heard this same song again being played on one of their local radio stations. It was then that I learnt that it had been written by a *Nancye Short Tsapralis*, an original member of *"The Archers"* one of Contemporary Christian music's' earliest groups in the United States of America. This song combines energetic

---

1 ©1977 John T Benson Publishing Co. Inc. / ASCAP

piano and tight harmonies with a strong bass line and featured on their *Fresh Surrender* album recorded in 1977. This young man, anointed by God and empowered by the Holy Spirit, connected my heart with God through his song in a very new way. I sang it with all of my heart, and at the end of his song, the young man shared the gospel message. Asking all who wanted to receive God's eternal life through repentance from sin, and trusting in the sacrifice and salvation offered through Jesus Christ, to raise their hands to pray and receive Jesus, he led us to our salvation experience. I joined in and prayed, although I did not know the full meaning of my actions at the time or what would change about my life. With this genuine heartfelt repentance and prayer, I was instantly spiritually born again. Through God's amazing divine setups, I would have the very pleasant surprise of meeting the young man who shared that message and led us in prayers many years later in England. He had also left Nigeria to become a pastor and later bishop of a very fruitful denomination, the late Bishop Gbenga Titus David. He is now with the Lord.

⌒⁂⌒

Unfortunately, my parents not yet saved themselves and with no additional knowledge or discipleship, my outward life continued as normal. I was not informed enough to know that I should read the scriptures daily or pray, which are the second most important principles of a life of faith. Beginning a walk with and better knowing God requires these two steps, without which we will be completely ignorant of our new spiritual status in and with God. Being the tender age of twelve and not yet feeding my new faith with God's word (the Bible), my life continued back on its usual track with no immediate sign or fruit of my new experience. I, however, was quickened in my heart by who I now recognize as the Holy Spirit to enroll in baptismal classes at my local Baptist church, where I had attended Sunday school. After successfully completing the classes, I was baptized at a big ceremonial event held in the same congregational hall of the church in which I had been saved. I did not fully realize until the day of the service, when it all fully dawned on my twelve-year-old mind, that baptism was a cornerstone doctrine for this denomination.

Baptists took baptism very seriously. I was, therefore, very surprised upon my arrival at the special service to see many families gathered, dressed in beautiful outfits, to attend their loved ones' baptisms and afterward take photographs with them. Although I shared with and invited my parents to the service, no one in my immediate family had any awareness of the significance of the spiritual events that had taken place in my life, so at my baptism I was the only one from my family in attendance. My father had gone out on some business, my mother was having her much-needed afternoon nap, and my siblings were outside playing. God was very present, however, and He made it a very special moment in my heart. I was baptized by the Rev. T. A. Akande and given an official church baptismal certificate confirming my new faith, which I still dearly cherish.

Chapter Three

COLLEGE DAYS BEGIN

With great gratitude to my educator parents, I successfully graduated from high school and completed all admission requirements and matriculation examinations for entrance into university at a younger-than-average age. I gained entrance into the University of Ife, Ile Ife, Nigeria (now known as the Obafemi Awolowo University), as one its youngest new undergraduate students. By age sixteen, having completed my GCE O levels early, topping them up with high WAEC (West African Examinations Council) and JAMB (Joint Admissions and Matriculation Board) examination scores, I was already in the university. A whole new and scary world of becoming an adult opened up to me. After surviving registration for my 101 classes, accompanied by my fervent mother (who, by the way, got into a heated verbal exchange with my prospective philosophy professor), I was ready to call it a day on my first visit to the university campus.

The lecturer had challenged and rebuked my mother for not letting me complete the registration process on my own. He said that many other students did so, and so could I! He stated that I now needed to more or less stop being attached to my mother's apron strings and start growing up! Mother disagreed with him strongly and told him so. Probably because of my younger-than-the-norm entrance age, she had insisted on being there for my class registrations to assist my smooth transition into college. I stayed out of their argument and enrolled in all my classes, and Mother finally returned home, leaving me on my own on campus at my new residence, Mozambique Hall, room 1.

This was one of the many dormitory rooms set apart for new students, who were humorously nicknamed Jambites, after the JAMB examinations we all had to pass to gain admission into the university. The first night on the college campus went peacefully until I heard some very loud shouting very early the next morning. It sounded like a war had broken out there. I was all alone; my other roommates had not yet arrived. I was so scared that I quickly got up and rushed to hide in a corner, missing the familiar and safe surroundings of my family's residence. I quietly waited for the noise to die down so I could find out what the disruption was all about. Later in the day, I had to laugh out loud when I finally ventured out to take a look and was informed that this was the "Man o' War" students group doing their very strict, early-morning, military-style exercises, which included marching routines. College life had begun in earnest!

My first set of college roommates were truly a bevy of beauties, and one of them, Rita Martins, won the Miss

Nigeria beauty pageant in 1982. There were a couple of Christians in the large dorm room, but they made no impact on me during the time shared in our residence hall. My diligent parents would visit every two weeks, bringing me news of my siblings and the rest of the family. I always looked forward to seeing them, having my groceries replenished, and receiving an allowance toward meals, books, and so on. They would also give food items to all my grateful roommates.

Rushing to early morning classes, grabbing seats in various lecture rooms and theaters, sitting through all manner of uninteresting academic information, and having to complete assignments to the satisfaction of cranky professors made life in college a far cry from my fun-filled elementary and high-school days. On the weekends was when all the fun would begin with my new college friends. I soon settled into a new routine, with my previous spiritual experiences pushed to the back of my mind by my new responsibilities and social gatherings with my newly acquired, "unsaved" companions.

During semester breaks, going on vacation trips to London was the in thing to do for middle-class Nigerian families, so off to London I would go to visit with family and friends whenever the college campus was closed.

Chapter Four

THINGS FALL APART

A very rude awakening shocked and interrupted all of our busy lives in the early to mid-1980s. Nigeria suddenly underwent a military takeover of the democratically elected government. Military forces had overthrown the government in place and had taken over power. Great political unrest followed. Fear permeated the air as the unrest began, accompanied by a very deep economic recession. The nation quickly descended into a serious economic crisis.

Prior to this governmental change, both my parents had been educators by career, but my mother retrained in mass communication, working for many years at the Federal Radio Corporation of Nigeria. Her voice and diligent work ethic led to her carving a niche for herself as a presenter, producing and hosting a highly popular Yoruba morning talk show titled *Pirilolongoji*. The then-governor of her state (Oyo state), Bola Ige, personally sent her a letter of commendation on the great success and popularity of her show. Also filling in as a news anchor, she later went on to television as an actress. One of her final works on television was a major role in a drama produced by one of Nigeria's well-known Christian production companies. Her lovely singing voice had also earned her a spot on the Federal Radio Corporation of Nigeria's national choir, performing all over the country with them as well as in her local church's choir. Our father stayed in his field as an educator, and for many years was the chairperson for various organizations and parents and teachers associations. Born to a very wealthy but largely Muslim family, my father had converted to Christianity early in his life. This contributed to a complete separation from his well-to-do family and resulted in many great hardships for him. He would later become very active in and for his local church and various Christian organizations and ministries.

Worth a mention at this point for the important role this fact was about to play and would continuously play in the life of every Nigerian is that Nigeria is one of the world's largest oil-producing countries. With a maximum crude oil production capacity of 2.5 million barrels per day, Nigeria ranks as Africa's largest producer of oil and the sixth-largest oil-producing country in the world. The nation also appears to have a greater potential for gas than oil. The management of this great wealth of energy resources and the nation's economy as a whole was about to greatly impact my family's individual story and that of all of the country's citizens.

Generally, the economy performed well when worldwide oil prices were booming, but the opposite effect was sharply felt almost instantly when prices fell. Having been so blessed with this one rich source of our nation's wealth, our leaders had failed to develop other potential wealth-building sectors of the nation's economy. There were about 180 million people in Nigeria in 2012. In twenty-five years, that number is expected to rise to 300 million people according to the UN— that's the current population of the United States fitting roughly into an area double the size of California. Being Africa's most populous nation, the past mismanagement of Nigeria's great wealth and resources has the potential to destabilize a great number of people in the continent of Africa. The artificial state of penury created in the nation by many years of alleged deep corruption and wealth mismanagement has been and continues to be a mystery and source of overwhelming misery to many Nigerians.

My paternal grandfather was from the Owu people, a part of the Yoruba tribe in Nigeria. He finally settled in a town called Gbongan, in Osun State, Nigeria, building the family's wealth on what was a vast cocoa-exporting business in the old western region of Nigeria. The family were the business tycoons of their time, involved in cocoa production and the transportation business. Their agricultural business prospered and expanded from Gbongan to Ibadan. The transportation business also prospered and spread its tentacles from Gbongan to Ife, Ilorin, Ilesa, Ofa, Ibadan, and other towns in the western region of Nigeria. From this base, my grandfather was able to give his children the best education available at the time in Nigeria and England, producing a line of educators, senior advocates of Nigeria (i.e., Nigeria's highest ranking lawyers), architects, and a supreme court justice on our nation's highest judicial bench.

Another of the nation's most valuable untapped resources is the wealth of rich soil that covers most of the country; hence the double green colors in the Nigerian flag, symbolizing agriculture. My parents, being passionate and optimistic about the nation's future, had decided to take the very bold step of investing in her economy by reviving part of their family's great agricultural heritage. This was all prior to the sudden latest bout of political and economic unrest. Reestablishing the family's prosperous agricultural and other businesses was their vision as they retired from their careers early. After a lot of research, they finally took on their new roles as entrepreneurs. They invested most of their acquired wealth in a major acquisition of land for the venture and purchased various agricultural resources. Additional funding for their efforts also came in from wealthy friends, partners, and banks. Having procured equipment, hired needed staff, and received extra help from all of our immediate and extended family members to clear land, set up new buildings, and obtain all manner of necessary equipment, the new company opened its

doors. They quickly settled into private business owner-
ship after a homestead for our family was completed.

Distribution and sales channels opened across
many cities, and various poultry and other organic produce became the products of their new poultry and agricultural company named Olu's Green Fields in Ajoda
New Town, Nigeria. The business was named after the
beginning of my dad and mum's first names. Eventually
my parents moved our family from our familiar city life,
family, and friends to resettle us in this new resort-like
area, a suburb of the city of Ibadan, in Oyo state. For
my siblings and me, assisting them in every little way
was a source of joy and pride as this was the new family
business. We no longer needed to shop for much of our
groceries. The freshest produce came from our farming
section daily. Fruits (I loved the delicious fresh papaya
and guavas), various vegetables, eggs, chicken, and fish
from the pond at the edge of the land surrounding the
homestead all became "free" for us!

My parents were extremely generous. Family members and friends who stopped by any time were always
blessed with abundant supplies of free, fresh produce
from the farm. Later, their generosity would also benefit
my roommates as I went off to college. They would regularly give fresh eggs to my roommates every time they
visited my campus dormitory room.

They also decided that our mother should obtain
visas and travel to Germany and the United States to

learn more about the latest agricultural and other technologies that could be applied back home in Nigeria. Their intention was to raise awareness of this untapped resource in our nation, contribute to the country's economic success, and establish new partnerships abroad. The business took off and was booming until that latest bout of governmental upheaval again shook and destabilized the country. Inexperienced investors, like my parents, who had taken on the extremely high risk of investing substantially large amounts of capital to conduct business in an unstable economic and political system, were hit the hardest. The very immediate effect of the fast-descending recession was felt in all sectors of the Nigerian economy. Burgeoning businesses that supported the nation's prosperity and provided jobs for many suffered, falling into rapid decline. With the financial crisis, the value of the Nigerian currency (the naira) plummeted, and before my parents could complete the second phase of their plan, the Nigerian economic bubble had once again burst and the nation's finances turned for the worst. I was in the midst of completing my university degree. Our family life would never be the same again.

A mass exodus of Nigerians, young and more mature alike, immediately began in earnest, with many escaping to Europe and other nations to rebuild their lives and find new sources of wealth and opportunities. Understandably demoralized, a great spiritual and economic darkness enveloped my parents as they scrambled to recover their rapidly disappearing capital, repay debts, and figure out new ways to support both our immediate and extended family members, staff workers, and all who depended on them.

The ripple effect on my life as they muddled through became a whirlwind of commuting between my university studies in Nigeria and quick trips to London, taking on odd jobs to support my two siblings who had been living in London for their academic studies. A third sibling, Kolade, would later join us. Not only could we no longer depend on our parent's financial support for tuition, accommodation, transportation, meals, and so forth, the choice of returning home to Nigeria was no longer an option. All of our very young lives were deeply traumatized by the new realities. From being a regular teenager with accompanying needs and my own university expenses, I was forced to take on the more than Herculean task of trying to graduate and help support the family. What seemed like a crushing weight was suddenly largely thrust upon my young shoulders. Managing to graduate in the midst of this unfolding turmoil was nothing short of a miracle, but with God's help, and I give Him all the credit, I obtained my university degree. I graduated from the faculty of Arts, University of Ife, in Ile Ife, Nigeria.

Chapter Five

GOD'S FAITHFULNESS

Upon graduating, I had become quite resolute about assisting my family through the fast-mounting financial distress all around. With that mindset, I completed all the necessary paperwork, and 1986 found me standing in line at the hot, non-air-conditioned at that time, Muritala Mohammed International Airport in Lagos. Joining many others, I was making a permanent exit from Nigeria to begin a completely new life. My destination was the United Kingdom and, unlike my previous vacation visits, I was headed back to London as a teenage college graduate with no parental support and siblings to care for. The only family friends willing and able to offer guidance were located in the East End of London, so the new journey to learn to survive on our own for my siblings and me began in the friendly and industrious area of East London.

When leaving Nigeria, an inexplicable peace and unshakable confidence in God had enveloped my heart. Although I was being propelled solely and wholly by my family's need to survive, faith in the knowledge that God was traveling with me had somehow been embedded deep inside my heart through his Holy Spirit. I

became aware of His great love and concern for us as a
family and believed that He would make my way prosperous. This deep, abiding faith had been initiated in
me by God through a verse of scripture I had come to
learn: "The earth is the LORD's, and everything in it,
the world, and all who live in it" (Psalm 24:1, NIV).
I received this verse as a personal prophecy from the
Lord. If I believed that the whole earth and the world
belonged to Him, including all who lived in it, which
included my family and me, then we could go anywhere
in the world and expect to be under the care of His
eternal, mighty, and everlasting arms.

I am unable to recall who taught me the verse or
how I came to know it, but the words became strong
and clear in my heart, building my faith to receive God's
help for the upcoming journey during the preparation
for my departure. I had heard, believed, and received
this word as a personal promise from God to me. Later
on, as I encountered many difficulties, tears, and fears, I
would remind myself of, pray, and meditate on this one
verse over and over again. By God's own compassion-
ate intervention, He had released a *key principle of faith*
to me: that faith is always first initiated by God's word
coming to us. When we respond by receiving, believing,
and firmly fixing our faith in His word, we will starve
all our doubts to death.

Although I was not yet fully trained in God's word,
still very clueless as to what being a Christian and how

to live as one fully meant, I had been guided by God to a very important principle of living by faith. This was the first of many faith lessons to come on my journey. It is of supreme importance for us to understand that faith is not built upon the strength of our needs, adversities, willpower, experiences, or ideas. The intensity of our desire to receive or acquire God's assistance during any given situation is not enough to produce faith. Our needs alone, great and sometimes dire as they may be—such as the healing of terminal diseases, addictions, financial breakthroughs, relationship ills—will not by themselves produce the victorious faith in God that we so crave. For faith in God to be truly birthed, nurtured, and victorious, we must aggressively pursue and expose our minds and hearts to God's word (the Bible) on a daily basis. This seeking after God through His word and prayers will result in an encounter with Him and His word that releases from the vast resources of the scriptures specific prophetic responses to our particular circumstances.

So then faith cometh by hearing, and hearing by the word of God. (Romans 10:17; italics added)

How then shall they call on him in whom they have not believed? (Romans 10:14, KJV)

Faith is birthed and nurtured through this divine process in our hearts by first hearing the word of God, receiving it, fully trusting in and getting that word established in our hearts, and then confidently acting upon our belief in that word. For our faith to grow, we must continue to be nurtured by the word of God, our "sword of the spirit." The outcome of our confident assurance in God, whatever His answer to us is, will be what the Bible calls "good success."

> This Book of the Law shall not depart from your mouth, but you shall meditate on it day and night, so that you may be careful to do according to all that is written in it. For then you will make your way prosperous, and then you will have good success. (Joshua 1:8, ESV)

The sharing of this principle of genuine Christian faith is one of my key reasons for writing this memoir and sharing my journey of faith with you. I hope to be able to play a very small part in sparing others the trial and error that a desperate soul may engage in when circumstances become extremely difficult. I endeavor to spare and help as many as possible to avoid the crushing sense of defeat and disappointment that may ensue when our desperate pleas seem to be unheeded.

If our expectations are not built on the assurance of faith that is found in hearing, receiving, and acting upon *all* of God's promises in His word alone, we will encounter and experience many spiritual and other failures. Although God's compassion is very great and he may sometimes sovereignly intervene in our circumstances with acts of mercy, this alone will not give us, His believing children, the consistent access to divine assistance that we all need. God strongly desires to meet our needs, and we so desperately need him in our most difficult moments, but He acts based on His word, so to experience His divine hand in our lives, we must connect our needs to God's word. Increasing our knowledge of the *power* that lies in God's word and strengthening our understanding of where our victory in Christ lies, we can prevent presumptuous actions that can negatively impact our walk with God. Redemption comes to us all, beginning with acknowledging our sinful condition, placing our trust (faith) in God's forgiveness of our sins, and receiving the saving grace that He offers through the sacrificial death and resurrection of His Son, Jesus Christ. This must then be followed by diligent discipleship in God's word (the Bible). A continuous learning of faith principles from the scriptures will prevent us from mistaking our presumptions for true faith, preventing the losses that ignorance of God's word and ways may have brought to many Christians. "My people are destroyed from lack of knowledge." (Hosea 4:6, NIV)

Chapter Six

CANON BY PACHELBEL

Having now permanently relocated to London from Nigeria, my siblings and I moved several times to any available and affordable part of town, while I continued my meager financial support for them. Work, further studies, and other opportunities were all open possibilities but now very distant goals as the first was survival! The years following my move were full of tremendous and overwhelming struggles. Wondering how our parents were doing, paying for our accommodations and my siblings' tuition, daily fears and worries, hoping no one fell ill, wondering how to put food on the table, and purchasing weekly bus and train passes for everyone to get to school and work was no easy feat as we all daily commuted from one end of town to the other, comprising almost unforgettable nightmares for us. Added for me was the task of attending my siblings' parent–teacher conferences and school events, and facing the mounting criticisms of our parents by family, friends, and peers who were puzzled as to why our lives had suddenly become unraveled. All manner of traumas and survival dramas became my daily routine.

Adjusting quickly to a whole new life without the presence of our very strong energetic and resourceful mother and our doting father was especially brutal for the dear younger ones. Our parents mostly could only support us with their fervent prayers, long-distance phone calls (this was before cell phones became so accessible to all), and many words of encouragement. They had let go of most of their staff, did most of the work themselves, and wrestled daily with their new circumstances on the home front. Today, looking back, I commend their fortitude, tenacity, and unwavering determination. They never quit, and I don't recall hearing either parent ever speak of giving up, though they were now in extremely dire straits. They worked tirelessly and relentlessly to the end, believing in God's ability to bring them through. Because of their great tenacity, although they had lost all of their own capital investment, they were able to pay back every creditor and did not lose any of the many acres of land they had purchased and owned. Upon their passing, they were able to leave all of that real estate as an inheritance for their children.

Both of my parents became born-again Christians some years after this very dark period. After this fresh encounter with God, they both rededicated all of their land to God, renaming it God's Green Fields. Our father then began to work tirelessly, serving the Lord in his local church. Many other ministries and Christian organizations also benefitted from his zeal and dedication to Christ's service. He succeeded in assisting one of the largest ministries in the nation, the Sword of the Spirit Ministries, also known as Christ Life Church, founded by Bishop Francis Wale Oke and headquartered in Ibadan, Nigeria, in acquiring much of the land for many of their major buildings.

The purpose of sharing the good news of and spreading the Gospel of our Lord Jesus Christ now became his and our mother's sole daily focus. The most impressive part of the real estate acquisitions he helped the church to purchase was the speed with which he could get things done. The purchases with which he was involved were always completed in record time. He devoted great attention to every paperwork detail, processing each with honesty, accountability, and transparency. This accomplishment was unusual and was no small achievement, as the purchase of any real estate in Nigeria was subject to extremely long delays and many scams, while many officials would demand large bribes before being willing to do the job for which they were paid. This was largely due to the extremely high level of corruption in the nation at the time. We all now believe that God must have especially anointed him for this special service during that period in order to further His purposes on the earth. Many dark and trying moments from this very difficult period of all of our lives are hard to forget, but one will forever stand out in my memory.

It involved a piece of music that I doubt I will ever be able to listen to again without tears welling up: Pachelbel's "Canon in D Major." It is the name commonly given to a piece of music by the German Baroque composer Johann Pachelbel in his "Canon and Gigue for Three Violins and *Basso Continuo*." The occasion was an end-of-year school event at my brother Muyiwa's high school in south London. He was being honored with an award for doing so well, and I had rushed through an extremely busy workday to be there to support and watch him receive the award. At some point during the evening's program, I heard this memorable piece of music for the very first time. It was their high-school band playing Pachelbel's canon. It might have been sheer exhaustion on that dark, cold, winter night, combined with memories of my parents and how our family used to be, or some other thought, but suddenly I was overwhelmed by a great wave of sadness. Struggling quietly not to break into loud sobs that would have startled the people sitting on both sides, embarrassing my young brother, and disrupting the program, I struggled as I sat through the entire piece. The realization of how much my parents had lost hit home hard as they were not here to see how well their son was doing.

As the piece played its lovely repetitive sound, my distress at how much we had lost as a family only grew. The deepest sense that we had lost not only our economic status but our oneness and identity as a unit had never been greater than in that moment and on that day. At the time I also did not know that my brother Muyiwa would never see our father alive again. I felt totally spent energy-wise—my very long, dark hair, for which I had been quite famous on my college campus—began to fall out—but soldier on we all did. I was not yet as strong in gaining victory with the word of God as I would later learn and share with you on this journey. If I had been stronger in the word, I would have replenished myself in those early days with this faith lesson from His word:

> He gives power to the weak
> and strength to the powerless.
> Even youths will become weak and tired,
> and young men will fall in exhaustion.
> But those who trust in the Lord will
> find new strength.
> They will soar high on wings like eagles.
> They will run and not grow weary.
> They will walk and not faint. (Isaiah 40:29–31,
> NIV)

My understanding and thinking would later be revolutionized as I learned how to wrestle and gain victory over life's circumstances with the word of God. In God's word are the keys to our source of all the power that we will ever need to live, share, and proclaim the Gospel of the Lord Jesus Christ. Credit must, however, again be offered to God as he revealed Himself as a helper again and again during our tremendous struggle, in answer to many prayers through a local church that had a strong emphasis on youth ministry. Generous members of their congregation offered help and support for my two brothers from their own resources, becoming surrogate parents to my two younger brothers. My struggling, lonely, young siblings were extremely grateful for their assistance, especially the older of my two younger brothers, who was able to start part-time work while completing his studies. He began to contribute support for himself and our youngest brother. My younger sister and I also continued to muddle through. "Blessed to be a blessing" is another Christian principle that was fully practiced by this precious congregation, whose rewards can only be measured out by the Lord himself.

> Whoever brings blessing will be enriched, and one who waters will himself be watered. (Proverbs 11:25, ESV)

> Besides, God is able to make every blessing of yours overflow for you, so that in every situation you will always have all you need for any good work. (2 Corinthians 9:8, ISV)

A few years later, after offering fervent prayers regarding the future of my youngest brother, Kolade, who was later renamed Bolaji, I gained fresh wisdom from the Lord. He revealed to me that my brother's life and God-endowed destiny would only fully blossom if I trusted Him (the Lord) with it. Assuring me of his full protection over his life, He strongly and gently prompted me to allow Bolaji to return home to our parents in Nigeria. This was at first not a welcome idea to any one of us because my two brothers were extremely close and did not want to be separated. Having been reunited in London, the four of us became the only cohesive family unit we had left, so we did not wish to be torn apart I also, in addition to the many hardships, would have had to purchase a very expensive plane ticket for him to go back to Nigeria.

God again revealed Himself as a wonderful helper, raising all of the necessary funds and helping me to overcome both my parents' and many of his local church leaders' extremely strong resistance to his return. Thus, Bolaji safely returned to our parents in Nigeria. Today, as God had promised, he has become a household name and well-known minister of the Gospel of our Lord Jesus Christ in Nigeria and abroad. Both my younger brothers, having overcome many trials and hardships, have gone on to become highly successful. To date, they both continue to express profuse gratitude to and show their support for the wonderful local congregation that shared the love of God with them and took them in during this time of great need.

Chapter Seven

HOPE RENEWED

A few more years went by before I could finally move out of our shared residence, relocating to begin life on my own at my humble new abode in Pimlico, a very serene part of London SW1.

I quickly landed a job through a referral set up by a family friend, working for an insurance company. Months later, in what can only be described as another act of God's undeniable intervention through a newspaper job advertisement, I was recruited by and began a new position at the Kabel Halsey financial services group, based in the financial district called the City of London. My new boss at the company offered initial and ongoing training, so I began in my new career as a trainee financial consultant.

Not too long after joining the company, the two principal directors of the group decided to part ways. They split the company into two new financial entities, and I went off with one half of the group to the newly formed brokerage firm, A J Blake & Associates at their new offices in Denmark Street, London WC2. Having witnessed at close range how one's life status can be altered so swiftly and dramatically, I had lost a lot of my God-endowed confidence, so working in London's financial district was beyond any of my wildest dreams at that point. I counted this new job among the many blessings from God and an undeniable witness to me of the faithful care He had promised when I left Nigeria for good. This was yet another miracle on my journey of faith. The years I spent at A J Blake & Associates are part of my fondest career memories, filled with unforgettable lunch and dinner events, sponsored by our very generous boss, at many of London's best restaurants.

After a quick commute to work, my mornings began with a hot cocoa from the deli across the street, followed later in the day with lunch at a pasta place called *Fatsos* with my new colleagues. Their extremely generous portions would place us in a food fog almost on the verge of a coma, and then we would all head back to the office. We each had our favorite eateries in and around London's Soho district; mine was a wonderful Chinese restaurant in the area. Evening drinks after work with colleagues who had now become friends would end the day (strictly no alcohol for me), with lots of chatter about setting me up on dates, whining about difficult clients, and so forth. Oh, we had so much fun! Life was full and busy, with seemingly endless appointments and meetings all over town, building the financial portfolios of our clients. We always looked forward to the end-of-quarter events to celebrate and award our star performers as they took place at some of London's swankiest restaurants. The best part of the year was the Christmas season, with lavish parties sponsored by our generous boss, Adrian. Dressed in all our finery, it was a wonderful turnaround for me from the previous traumatic years.

I worked tirelessly, continuing to partially support my family, and was rewarded with managing part of the financial portfolios for some very well-heeled clients, one of whom was the famed Nigerian industrialist, the founder of Adegoke Group of Companies, the late Chief (Elder) Amos Olasupo Adegoke, based in Ibadan Nigeria. . I was promoted and soon became one of the team leaders in our company. This meant even more fun on the job, including one-on-one lunch meetings with the boss and, the best part, access to a program assisting in the purchase of our first home! So some months after my promotion, I was able to purchase my very first home: a beautiful flat in Croydon. I also bought myself a new car. The previous years' agonies begin to fade away, and life again settled into a happier rhythm. Finally things were looking up!

I loved my new home on Brampton road in Croydon. It was a quiet little haven from my hectic work schedule and just the right size for me. I had also become a very active member of a newly formed local church congregation introduced to me by one of my financial services clients who worked at the Commonwealth Secretariat office in London. Grateful to God for all that He had done and loving Him with all my heart, I wanted to express my heart toward Him through worship and service to Him. I was usually the very first to arrive for the Sunday morning worship service and would join their new pastor to set up the congregational meeting hall for the service. I was also one of the last ones to leave. Soon I became the volunteer choir leader and children's Sunday school teacher, and served in any other odd jobs needed by the new group. This drove me to seek God more through the scriptures so that I could better know and serve Him. All was, however, not perfect in my world. During the previous nightmarish years spent with my siblings, I had met and dated a non-Christian young fellow in my ignorance of another of God's faith principles.

> Do not be yoked together with unbelievers. For what do righteousness and wickedness have in common? Or what fellowship can light have with darkness? (2 Corinthians 6:14, NIV)

Therefore, unfolding alongside my new wonderful life was an increasingly unpleasant dating experience. It was proof and a lesson in my young Christian walk that ignorance and violation of God's word will not spare us the consequences of wrong belief systems and actions. We, however, have a merciful and forgiving God who continually reveals His loving kindness and tender mercies to us without fail, and I was yet again about

to experience His amazing grace in the midst of my
spiritual ignorance, deep emotional unhappiness, and
inconsistent Christian walk. Halleluiah! God brought a
handsome, fervent young Christian man to our church!
His name? Jide.

Jide had been born and raised in West London and
spent a few childhood years in London, but then had
returned to live with his parents in Nigeria. His parents
had lived in London, completed their studies and training there, and then returned with their young children
to their homeland. Jide had lived in Lagos, Nigeria, until
becoming an adult, attending Maryland Comprehensive
Secondary School in Lagos and then completing his
university degree as a pharmacist at the University of
Ibadan in Nigeria. He had decided to return to London
to further his studies and career and, upon his arrival,
met our young local pastor and was now living in North
London. A fervent disciple of the word of God, his love
for God was clearly evident to all. He was soon being
asked by the elders of our church to share Sunday morning sermons with the congregation. I was very impressed
with his humility and the unabashed swiftness with
which he would kneel down to pray.

Being already extremely passionate about God, I
was deeply hungry for more knowledge of His word and
had begun to seek answers to fix my unhappy Christian
walk. I was drawn to this young man's confident knowledge of the scriptures. We developed a friendship, and

he invited me to attend a midweek Bible study group, so after work, we would all gather to learn from the scriptures with some other young Christians. Sometime later, during the summer months, the church hosted a visit to London from the founding pastor of the church who resided in Lagos, Nigeria. He was coming to support the new London congregation. Jide and I were asked to serve together in various capacities during this special event, so we got to know each other well. I also found out that I had attended the same university in Nigeria as his sister and that we had friends in common from our college days.

Through various church encounters, a lot of praying, and some unexpected matchmaking work of the Holy Spirit, it came as quite a shock to us both, but nonetheless a happy surprise, to slowly discover God's plan for us to get married. He proposed to me, we called our parents to inform them, and went to our church leaders to receive their blessings. All went well, so the following year, on a lovely spring day that also happened to be his birthday, I had the wonderful privilege of marrying this wonderful, God-honoring man. We became one as a family and had the joy of having many members of our family and friends in attendance.

"For this reason a man will leave his father and mother and be united to his wife, and the two will become one flesh" (Ephesians 5:31, NIV). A brand-new chapter in our lives began to unfold, and we quickly settled into our married life. Building a new family comes with its own unique set of joys, challenges, and ups and downs. This beautiful, God-ordained, lifetime union between a man and woman is a huge responsibility and not to be entered into lightly. When done God's way, it leaves no room for exits and requires one's full devotion and, sometimes, many unexpected sacrifices to succeed. I am forever grateful to God and feel so very fortunate to say that my precious-beyond-words husband has been and continues to be a very special blessing from God in my life. As I write this faith memoir more than two decades after that glorious wedding day, he has grown to become an even more devoted witness for the Lord Jesus Christ. A deeply humble, committed, faithful, and loving spouse, he continues to be a delight. I had again been blessed by God with more than I could ever have asked Him for.

Chapter Eight

GOD'S DESTINY FINDS YOU

I t was springtime the following year after our marriage, and I was heavily pregnant with our first child. My delivery due date was less than a week or so away when a very unusual request came in from my voice teacher, Kathleen Bentley. Over the years, I had regularly taken classical vocal training in order to better fulfill my choir and worship leader responsibilities. She had suddenly decided and became quite adamant about entering me in a major talent competition that was taking place in a few days. I wondered why she would make such an absurd request, knowing that I was soon to give birth, and I strongly resisted. Kathleen would not give up the idea; I guess she may have thought that I would have even less time once the baby was born. This major regional music festival took place annually, and she insisted that she did not want me to miss that year's opportunity. I thought it all strange but, extremely reluctantly, I went along with her idea, feeling and looking all of nine months pregnant. Nervous upon arrival, as I had not really prepared for this, I faced the panel of judges and sang my selected gospel numbers. I was stunned after my performance to receive their highest award for vocal talent at the Coulsdon and

Purley Festival. My teacher was right and had believed in me when I thought I was not ready.

The very next day, a week before the first anniversary of our marriage, we were blessed with our first child, a beautiful daughter we named Ebunoluwa (meaning gift of God in our Nigerian Yoruba language). Staying at home to recover and care for her, the maternity leave months flew by fast. It was soon time to return to work. Being parted from my new baby proved to be more difficult than I had imagined or planned for. Most working mothers come to discover this hard truth. After much prayer, obtaining and checking references, and trial and error with different childcare services, we hired a middle-aged lady to look after her. Trying not to worry about her safety and care all day long, I worked hard at the balancing act of wife, mom, and career woman. This arrangement, however, did not work out well for me.

Frequently, the caregiver would take independent actions that ignored our concerns and directives, and things soon deteriorated to the point of a lawsuit. We removed our daughter from her care and tried a few other options before I finally decided that I was done with leaving her in the care of others. Although many new moms and their families are able to make a smooth transition of returning to work, this was not the case for me. After consulting with my husband, who was also working, I resigned from my job to temporarily stay at home to look after Ebun. It was an extremely difficult decision income-wise, but for me not nearly as difficult as leaving her every morning in the care of strangers. This may not be an obtainable or desirable choice for everyone, but we both prayerfully decided it was the right call for our new family. Far from being a smooth transition, due to the big drop in our household income, it was, however, a great relief to know that she was safe and well cared for. Her safety as our priority gave us the much-needed strength to stick with the commitment we had made to God who had trusted us with this precious new one's life, and He has never failed us.

All grown up now, our beautiful daughter has become a God-honoring professional young lady and a great source of joy to us. In 2019, she received an award from the United States House of Representatives for her exceptional performance in her chosen career. We are always blessed to be identified as her parents. God had yet again fulfilled another of His promises and a principle of faith. He will take care of us when we surrender all to, and trust in Him.

> And this same God who takes care of me will supply all your needs from his glorious riches, which have been given to us in Christ Jesus. (Philippians 4:19, NLT)

> The LORD is my shepherd, I lack nothing. (Psalm 23:1, NIV)

The decision I made to become a stay-at-home mom, solely to resolve our childcare dilemma, would surprisingly prove to be a major turning point in all of our lives! We regularly attended our local church and had become used to our new family routines as our lives continued to move forward at a steady pace. Having served the Lord in so many different capacities in the past while I had been a single lady, I now had to devote most of my time to building our new family. Still, occasionally, my thoughts would wander as to how I could continue to serve God in light of my new responsibilities as wife and mother. One day, while expressing my heart to God fervently in prayer, I earnestly sought and yearned for an answer from Him regarding how I could continue serving Him with all my new responsibilities. Well, He must have been waiting for me to ask because faster than I could say amen, the answer to my prayers began to manifest.

The God-given talent to sing that I had never considered to be anything more than a gift of DNA from our multitalented parents was about to catapult me from career to calling! What for me had settled into a steady, pragmatic Christian walk was about to turn into a whole new level of serving God. Volunteering at my local church as an unmarried Christian had for me been easy and enjoyable. My new family life seemed to make that nearly impossible, but another word from the principles of faith in the scriptures would prove me wrong! That is, *nothing* is impossible with God.

For with God nothing shall be impossible.
(Luke 1:37, KJV)

Jesus looked at them and said, "With man this
is impossible, but with God all things are possible." (Matthew 19:26, NIV)

A short while after my simple prayer, and quite out
of the blue, I suddenly received an invitation to sing at
another local church's special event in London. I accepted
the invitation and prepared for the event. With less than
a hundred people in attendance (there weren't too many
mega churches in London back then), nothing appeared
to be out of the ordinary. We arrived at the location,
parked our car, and joined other invited guests and
members of the congregation gathered in the meeting
space for the service. Ushers guided us to our delegated
seats as we all chatted and greeted one another, waiting for the service to begin. After the opening prayers,
the host pastors greeted everyone and the service began.
Soon, I was next on the program and I got up, shared a
few words of greeting, and began to sing.

I was so immersed in the song, belting out a tune
for God with my eyes closed, that I did not immediately
notice that something unusual was happening. What I
can only describe today as a sovereign move of God suddenly began to unfold. The presence of God invaded the
room, and the atmosphere totally changed! The tangible

and undisputable presence of God filled the room, transforming the entire mood of the event. The pastor excitedly got up, followed by many others. Both he and they began shouting, dancing, clapping, and raising their hands, giving their uninhibited praises to God. Affirming shouts of "Amen!" and "Praise the Lord!" filled the air as they unashamedly rejoiced in God's presence. The people's hearts begin to be touched, and as my selection moved to slower worship songs, many begin to kneel and to cry.

I finished singing and the pastor got up and immediately proceeded to deliver a very powerful sermon. An altar call for prayers, repentance, salvation, and rededication to God followed without any further interruptions, announcements, or delays. The scenes that followed were both amazing and magnificent. Lives were being transformed as people repented, and many broken lives and relationships were touched by God, healed and restored to Him and to one another. Many became born again, and word soon spread among many local churches in London that something wonderful had occurred. A snowball effect began to take place. No one was more surprised than I at this unexpected and rapid turn of events. New and more invitations began to pour in for me to sing and share the gospel for various church events.

All manner of churches and denominations around the city invited me to come and participate in their events. This soon led to an invitation from across the seas. My life was again permanently changed. Singing and preaching the Gospel of our Lord Jesus Christ became my new full-time assignment from the Lord. This was not even close to what I'd imagined I'd be doing to serve God!

Blessed and surprised by God, I was dubbed the Anointed Singer and later was also called the Alleluia Lady. These names were on account of my passionate shouts of the praise word "alleluia" before or after I sang or preached. Many have told to me that as I ministered, it felt as if they were seated under "open heavens," and that they had experienced an overwhelming sense of God's presence. Other new experiences also begin to occur during this period. Although I played no musical instruments, I also received from the Lord the gift of songwriting, and I begin to write new worship and praise songs unto the Lord. This series of encounters, begun exclusively by God, was His amazing answer to my simplest of prayers, expressing my deepest desire to serve Him.

His divine interruption transformed all of our lives. The call into full-time ministry and the anointing that God had placed upon me would release not only me but my entire family. Before this divine encounter, as far as I am aware on our family tree, no one in the family had ever served the Lord in full-time ministry. Many members of my family, including my parents as shared earlier, would later become born again and give their all to God.

Here I humbly share another of the faith principles the Lord Jesus has taught me. *God's destiny finds us!* His divine interruptions transform our lives when we step out in faith, based on His word, completely trusting in and faithfully serving him wherever he has currently placed and positioned us. He comes suddenly, interrupting our lives with His divine destiny. I once heard someone describe it this way, "God is like nothing, nothing, nothing, BAM!"

In 1 Samuel 9, God's destiny found Saul as he diligently searched for his father's donkeys. Instead of finding the donkeys, he received a kingdom. God's destiny found David while he tended to and protected his father's flock. Destiny interrupted the young Virgin Mary as she went about her everyday duties. The list goes on and on: Moses while he tended sheep in Midian, Joseph in prison, Gideon full of fear threshing wheat in a winepress, Esther at her uncle Mordecai's home, and Peter with his brother Andrew as they operated a fishing business.

> Now as Jesus was walking by the Sea of Galilee, He saw two brothers, Simon who was called Peter, and Andrew his brother, casting a net into the sea; for they were fishermen. And He said to them, "Follow Me, and I will make you

fishers of men." immediately they left their nets and followed Him. (Matthew 4:18–19, ESV)

And it is impossible to please God without faith. Anyone who wants to come to him must believe that God exists and that he rewards those who sincerely seek him. (Hebrews 11:6, NLT)

Whatever you do, do your work heartily, as for the Lord rather than for men, knowing that from the Lord you will receive the reward of the inheritance. It is the Lord Christ whom you serve. (Colossians 3:23–24, KJV)

God shook up my life and the lives of many of his servants as they simply faithfully served Him at their tasks at hand. I share some of the details of this amazing journey with you with the hope that you will be inspired and encouraged to embrace the Lord Jesus Christ and offer Him obedience, worship, and adoration. Your life will *never* be the same again. An unending adventure of faith and wonder awaits you that will provoke you to give unceasing praise to God daily.

Chapter Nine

THE PROPHETIC
UNLOCKS DESTINY

Having also previously been blessed to receive the baptism of the Holy Spirit, I now found myself regularly operating in what the scriptures define as the gifts of the Holy Spirit: words of wisdom, knowledge, and especially the wonderful gift of prophecy. Life as I knew it would *never* be the same again. "In the last days," God says in Acts 2:17, "I will pour out my Spirit on all people."

> Your sons and daughters will prophesy, your young men will see visions, your old men will dream dreams. Even on my servants, both men and women, I will pour out my Spirit in those days, and they will prophesy. (Acts 2:17–18, NIV)

> Now about the gifts of the Spirit, brothers and sisters, I do not want you to be uninformed. You know that when you were pagans, somehow

or other you were influenced and led astray to
mute idols.

Therefore I want you to know that no one who
is speaking by the Spirit of God says, "Jesus
be cursed," and no one can say, "Jesus is Lord,"
except by the Holy Spirit.

There are different kinds of gifts, but the same
Spirit distributes them. There are different
kinds of service, but the same Lord. There are
different kinds of working, but in all of them
and in everyone it is the same God at work.

Now to each one the manifestation of the Spirit
is given for the common good. To one there is
given through the Spirit a message of wisdom,
to another a message of knowledge by means
of the same Spirit, to another faith by the same
Spirit, to another gifts of healing by that one
Spirit, to another miraculous powers, to another
prophecy, to another distinguishing between
spirits, to another speaking in different kinds
of tongues, and to still another the interpreta-
tion of tongues. All these are the work of one
and the same Spirit, and he distributes them to
each one, just as he determines. (1 Corinthians
12:1–9, NIV)

Let love be your highest goal! But you should also desire the special abilities the Spirit gives— especially the ability to prophesy. (1 Corinthians 14:1, NLT)

Things begin to move rapidly, and with baby in tow every weekend found my husband and me attending church services all over as more invitations poured in than I could keep up with. A few more months of these whirlwind activities went by until one day during the regular Sunday worship service at my local church, I began to sense a strong impression from the Holy Spirit to give my first gospel concert. After much prayer, we selected one of our local town halls in Wallington, Surrey, as the venue. We contacted and sent flyers to many churches and our local newspapers to advertise the concert titled, "Music in My Heart," after one of the very first songs I had written. Another one of God's out-of-the-blue blessings was soon to make me realize that God was unveiling a bigger plan than my mind could fathom.

After reporters from both our regional newspapers, *The Guardian* and *The Herald*, heard about the concert, they called and interviewed me. Feature articles about me and the event were printed in their widely circulated newspapers, publicizing the event beyond any advertising we could have purchased. This elevated the event to a whole new level. We began to receive more phone calls and many new inquiries until the hall was soon filled to capacity, with standing room only! Surprised by the success of our first event, we would put on more gospel concerts, the largest one being a Memorable Gospel Concert I headlined in November 1993, at the London City Temple with the Rev. Bazil Meade and the London Community Gospel Choir. They were one of England's most successful gospel choirs at that time. Their credits included royal performances for Her Majesty the Queen, concerts, videos, and studio recordings with a lengthy list of well-known artists including Puff Daddy, Mariah Carey, Sting, and Paul McCartney. The City Temple concert took place just a few weeks after the birth of our second child, a strong and handsome baby boy that we named Oluwaremilekun (meaning; God's source of comfort in our Nigerian Yoruba language).

As I continued to minister during the pregnancy of and after the birth of our second child, we received many invitations to minister in song at special events and conferences from a wide variety of churches and organizations, including the British Red Cross. Now we had two babies in tow as we went from venue to venue. Again, I thank the Lord daily for His wisdom and preparation for His destiny in our lives, giving me a wonderful husband and a very supportive family. These fresh encounters with God continued and would ultimately lead me into what would become a life of full-time ministry:

singing, preaching, and prophesying in the service of our Lord Jesus Christ.

Now is probably the right time to share with you another unusual happening that began to occur at the various services I took part in. "You! Lady sitting over there! I see you moving to North America." I looked around me to see who was being addressed. To my shock, those startling words were being directed at me and were spoken by the host of the gathering I was attending on that day. *What in the world is this strange lady talking about?* I thought to myself. She might as well be prophesying that I would go to the moon. It had never crossed my mind to desire to live in the United States; vacation maybe, because I had an uncle who resides in Maryland, but relocate again to a new country? Most definitely not.

This interesting new phenomenon would not stop and continued for the next year and a half or so. In almost every meeting I would attend, complete strangers would single me out and say, "I have a word for you from the Lord: You are moving to America." One of my brothers also came to visit with us one day and stated, "I dreamed and saw you spending dollars." These words sounded so strange to me that I was unable to register them at all, no matter how often I repeatedly heard them spoken. My husband, children, and I were all British residents. Having endured the arduous mountain of applications, fees, and paperwork to settle us all in the

United Kingdom, my mind was now totally closed to ever making another major and exhausting move like that ever again. I somehow shut out and strangely did not at all connect with the words being spoken over my life by such a crowd of witnesses. My exact thoughts were, *how odd that people keep saying this.* Can you believe how dumb spiritually one can be when one does not want to see or hear the truth of God's word staring one right in the face, even when He is so close that one can almost feel His breath? However, the Lord in His mercy knew exactly how He would alter my fixed-to-living-in-England mindset. How long it would take for Him to shatter this fortress in my mind and finally get through to me was known only to Him. He quite simply lovingly and gently chipped away at the stronghold of permanent UK residency that I had built in my mind and heart.

God's prophetic timing for me to make this move was, however, rapidly approaching and coming to a close. Time was, unbeknownst to me, fast running out for me to leap over this great faith chasm and cross over the oceans once again to meet His timetable and schedule for my life. Well, He decided to speed things up *big time,* seeing that I was both extremely clueless and a dedicated slow coach on this one matter! One night, just before going to bed as I was rounding up the day with my normal night prayers and devotions, I suddenly clearly heard the quietest solemn voice within me say, "Open

Job 33:14 and read it." At that moment, I certainly could not recall ever having read or noticed this part of the scripture in the book of Job before. This sort of occurrence had only happened to me once before, early in my Christian walk. I was quite rattled and startled and was also immediately very troubled.

First, I was startled because I just clearly heard an instruction that was definitely from a third party and, second, because my first quick thought about the book of Job was about the man who went through the most severe of biblical accounts of life's trials and I had no idea what that verse would say. With trembling hands, I reached for my Bible and found the following scripture: "For God speaks again and again, though people do not recognize it" (Job 33:14, NLT).

I called out loudly to my husband, Jide, telling him what had just happened. He was just as astounded but proceeded in his usual manner to calmly pray and encourage me with the scriptures. Check out how completely dull of hearing I had become on this matter: I did not at all connect the dots but instead began to search my heart for what it could possibly be that I was not hearing God about. I was completely blind to and ignoring the elephant in the room! Talk about being slow and on the verge of complete disobedience to God's clear command. We can certainly be deaf to God when we choose not to see, hear, or receive the word of the Lord that is so close to us!

Anyone with ears to hear should listen and understand! (Matthew 11:15, NLT)

Whoever has ears, let them hear. (Matthew 13:9, NIV)

The principle of faith to be learned here is how uncooperative we can become to God's leading, even when accompanied by supernatural encounters repeatedly confirming His word. Many times we don't see what we do not want to see, and see only what we do want to see. We may fall into deception and miss God's best if we repeatedly continue to hear and believe only what we have decided on. This can be especially dangerous when the Lord desires to give us new information, correct our understanding of doctrine and truth, or release our destinies to us. "If you are willing and obedient, you will eat the good things of the land" (Isaiah 1:19, NIV). Instead of my stubborn ineptness, my response should have been that of the Psalmist: "God has spoken plainly, and I have heard it many times: Power, O God, belongs to you" (Psalm 62:11, NLT). My response should have been like Mary's, the mother of Jesus, when the angel appeared to her regarding the supernatural conception and birth of Jesus. This young woman was so willing to receive the words given to her by the angel about her appointment with God's destiny for her life that her immediate response was and is the key to our faith's being released.

"Mary responded, 'I am the Lord's servant. May everything you have said about me come true.' And then the angel left her" (Luke 1:38, NLT).

It very, very slowly finally began to dawn on me and penetrate my closed psyche that God may really have wanted me to move to the United States, no kidding! This was however a very alarming and depressing thought for two main reasons. First was my inaccurate concept of American life, already shaped by their popular entertainment sector's depiction of the culture as immoral and violent. The second reason, as I had already touched on, was that I loved my life living in quaint old England where all the remainder of our family and friends were. I did not at all desire to leave. Having two young children, the US did not seem to me to be the ideal environment to raise them in the knowledge, love, and reverence for God. It seems that I knew more about what was best for them than the God who endowed me with them. What an irony! While many American Christians prayed that God would not send them to Africa, I had been praying and hoping that God was surely not serious about moving us to the US. Although many dreamed of moving to our great nation, I had not yet plugged in to the very special blessing God was giving me—the privilege to receive from Him the joy and liberty of being His kingdom citizen in the US.

Our children, whom I almost prevented (not unlike disobedient Israel) from entering the Promised Land, would both grow up in California, wonderfully "saved and safe" in God's awesome hands and loving care. The ones I was reluctant to entrust to the Lord's prophetic word now serve the Lord with all their hearts. More about this a little later; my faith lesson here is that the only safe place for us and our families to be is in the very center of God's will for our lives. Wow! He had all this in His heart for us, and we knew it not. What an awesome God and task. All that would be continually required from now on was hearing, knowing, and *promptly* obeying God's voice. There was yet another faith learning curve, not to be like the foolish Galatians in the scriptures, trying to engineer, manipulate, or manufacture the continuation and completion of a move begun by God in the "flesh."

> Are you so foolish? After beginning by means of the Spirit, are you now trying to finish by means of the flesh? (Galatians 3:3, NIV)

> Being confident of this, that he who began a good work in you will carry it on to completion until the day of Christ Jesus. (Philippians 1:6, NIV)

> He will sustain you to the end, so that you will be blameless on the day of our Lord Jesus Christ. (1 Corinthians 1:8, Berean Study Bible)

The scriptures and God's prophetic word would from this point on be first and last in how we would plan to live the rest of our lives. The biblical mandate to spread the gospel to many nations through all possible means became real to us in a fresh new way. This mandate in our understanding did not seem to apply to the US, as we thought the nation already had a great Christian presence on the world stage. With the seeming proliferation of gospel preachers in the States, this mission was a great puzzle to our minds. We were later appalled to find out that the nation was indeed undergoing the most intense cultural and moral decline with true believers undergoing great spiritual warfare, and that many had become apostate believers. There was a lot that had to be swiftly accomplished before it was too late to recover minds and hearts to and for Christ. Rescuing millions of souls from ending up in the dreadful place called hell eternally did not exclude Americans, so we committed ourselves to God, partnering with Him in accomplishing His great kingdom work globally and locally.

> For we are God's fellow workers. You are God's field, God's building. (1 Corinthians 3:9, ESV)

> And he said unto them, Go ye into all the world, and preach the gospel to every creature. He that believeth and is baptized shall be saved; but

he that believeth not shall be damned. (Mark 16:15–16, KJV)

Now that the Lord had finally got through to me, I had no idea when to begin this move to the United States or what part of this great and vast nation we were to move to. We quite simply continued to pray and seek the Lord for His counsel, guidance, provision, and favor to accomplish it all.

Chapter Ten

HONORING GOD'S SERVANTS

The star of this memoir is the Lord Jesus Christ and His glorious word. Having reiterated this truth, I believe it would still be appropriate to give honor to some of God's great servants in the faith. Many have given their all in Christ's service, and I am privileged that they have been part of my journey of faith. One such man of great faith is the General Overseer of the Redeemed Christian Church of God, Pastor E. A. Adeboye. As God's anointing and calling upon my life became more and more visible to many, God's presence permeated the atmosphere wherever I was privileged to participate. Invitations to minister at various special events for many churches, ministries, and organizations continued to pour in.

One such invitation to minister in song came in the summer of 1993 from the choir master of a newly founded Redeemed Christian Church of God (RCCG) Angel parish in Islington, London. The event was on a weekend in July and included a summer concert. Services were being held at the St. Mark's Church, Myddelton Square, London EC1, off Mylne Street, and many guests and ministers were on the program. I was at the time pregnant with our second child who would be born in early October of that year. This did not prevent the Lord from blessing me with this and so many other wonderful opportunities.

The following year, 1994, the same parish hosted a special visit from their General Overseer, Pastor E. A. Adeboye, from Nigeria. At the time he was visiting London with one of his spiritual sons, who had trained as a medical doctor and then became one of their pastors.

The choirmaster reached out to me again, but this time asked that I sing a very special song that I was completely unfamiliar with and said that their choir would be my backing singers. The song was titled "My Tribute," written by an artist I had also never heard of before— Andrae Crouch! Yes! I was one of the two people left on earth who had been singing all of his songs in church but had never noticed the name of this legendary gospel artist and songwriter at the end of all those songs. More of this amazing tapestry woven by God continued to unfold. I at first resisted the idea; yup, that's me again always quickly hearing and obeying God's voice, but the choirmaster gently and persistently persuaded me to sing this song. I now believe it was the precious Holy Spirit who nudged him to help me accomplish God's purpose. I finally agreed to do the event and rehearsed with their choir for the special visit from their founder. I was very nervous and prayed that I would not make any mistakes during the performance before this great servant of God, but all went gloriously well.

I have, over the two decades since that event, heard hundreds of sermons, but I have never forgotten the message Pastor Adeboye preached from Isaiah 60:1, "Arise, shine, for your light has come, and the glory of the LORD rises upon you (NIV). This precious servant of Christ imparted the word of God to all in a gentle, humble, and low-key style of preaching, delivering his very powerful and life-transforming message quite differently from the affectionately loud and boisterous Pentecostal way that I had become accustomed to. As a young Christian, I was impressed and was also curious as to why a man who appeared to have all that he needed would leave a warm, sunny country like Nigeria to brave the dark, cold London winter nights for the difficult task of church planting. He had been a former professor of mathematics with a successful academic career. I now understand, as a more mature believer, that a genuine love for the Lord Jesus Christ supplies grace to our hearts to give our all to and for Him.

After the service, it was arranged for me to meet with and receive prayers from him. He prayed some prophetic words over my life, and also blessed me with an honorarium, the most generous I had received until that point. Our God truly is an amazing God because some months after singing Andrae Crouch's song at that event, I would meet and have a lasting friendship with that famous songwriter until his passing in 2015, through his twin sister, Evangelist Sandra Crouch. They are two of gospel music's greatest servants. Additionally, as an update of God's continuing wonders as only He could perform them, in December of the year 2014, more than twenty years after that 1994 event, I would again be blessed to meet with and receive prayers from the General Overseer.

It was another of God's many miraculous interruptions. Due to a change in flight arrangements in December 2014, I had flown to Lagos, Nigeria, a few days early for some ministry invitations. One of the events was to be at the Christ Life Church in Ibadan, Nigeria. The special speaker for the Redeemed Christian Church of God year-end Great Shepherd Conference, Bishop Francis Wale Oke, unexpectedly invited me to minister in special songs at the event. Millions tuned in live worldwide through their many media outlets, as the RCCG, as it is now known, had exploded in massive growth since the overseer had endured those cold winter days that I remembered way back in London. The church sponsors some of the largest Christian gatherings and audiences worldwide and had founded parishes in almost every nation. This conference was not on my schedule, but it was on God's schedule for me in another one of His many amazing surprises. Something wonderful occurred at the time without my noticing.

In attendance at the RCCG camp was their usual crowd of multiple thousands, with millions more tuning in online and through television. There was more than one master of ceremonies during that evening's event, but I was especially blessed to be introduced and receive appreciation for my ministry from a man who, unbeknownst to me, would become renowned all over the nation of Nigeria and around the world: Professor Yemi Osinbajo. A few days after I sang at the event, all the world's media announced Professor Yemi Osinbajo as the vice presidential running mate for Nigerian presidential candidate, Muhammadu Buhari. Upon winning their historic first term elections he became the vice president of the Federal Republic of Nigeria.

I was again blessed on May 30, 2015, to be invited to celebrate the presidential inaugurations and travel with Bishop Francis Wale Oke, who was one of the main speakers during the National Cathedral services. Seated right across from the new vice president and his family at the cathedral, I rejoiced as my youngest brother Bolaji nicknamed Big B, led part of the worship. All I could say was, "Lord, thank you so very much for bringing us through." My other brother, Muyiwa, also interviewed the new vice president for his television program. But God was not yet done!

Unexpectedly and by divine arrangement on the following day, I was the beneficiary of a second invitation to the Aso Rock (Nigeria's White House equivalent) presidential villa chapel, completing the very special services. I received all these blessings from the Lord without any effort on my part. I have no words to express my gratitude to Him. I had not asked the Lord for any of the experiences that I am privileged to recount, nor did I know, during the great struggle to keep my family intact, what God would do. I had simply trusted and sought Him with *all* my heart and might, entrusting our family's circumstances to Him.

That is what the Scriptures mean when they say, "No eye has seen, no ear has heard, and no mind has imagined what God has prepared for those who love him" (1 Corinthians 2:9, NLT).

Chapter Eleven

1995, A PIVOTAL YEAR

E arly in 1995, with the support and encouragement from many Christian brothers and sisters, I began work on and completed my first gospel album, *Devotion*. This title was my heart's response to God's call upon my life, a promise to devote the rest of my life to honoring and serving Him. As the album drew close to completion, I had begun to contact many of the pastors and church leaders, who had become friends and supporters, to share news of the new project. One afternoon, I received a phone call back from one of the pastors, the late Doctor Tayo Adeyemi. He was then senior pastor of one of the new and upcoming churches in London, New Wine Church. This church, under his leadership, would later grow to become one of London's "mega churches." He invited me to minister in song at his church on the coming Sunday, but that was just a few days away!

He stated that they were hosting a very special guest speaker from Lagos, Nigeria, Pastor Tunde Bakare. I expressed my regret that I would have to decline the invitation, informing him that my husband would be giving the sermon on that Sunday at our local church, and I had to be there to watch over our two young children and support him while he preached. God's precious Holy Spirit moved mightily upon Pastor Tayo during that telephone conversation, and he insisted that I should come, saying they would arrange my child care for that Sunday, and that it was an opportunity he believed I was not to miss. He stated that this special servant of God, whom I'd never heard of, from Lagos, would be an important person for me to meet.

With the benefit of hindsight, I would be blessed to have recognized Pastor Tayo's prophetic insight back then. In 2011, many years after the event I am about to recount, this man of God, Pastor Tunde Bakare, was selected to be the vice presidential running mate for Nigerian president, Muhammadu Buhari. This was before Professor Yemi Osinbajo took over the position in 2015. Back to my phone conversation with Pastor Tayo: he emphasized that he believed it was a divine and rare opportunity regarding God's assignment and destiny for me to meet and connect with this highly sought-after, prophetic leader. Although I had never heard of this great man, I became persuaded, due to my deep respect for Pastor Tayo, and accepted his very kind invitation.

This phone call was to become the beginning of yet another series of wholly divine connections in my life. On the said Sunday, my husband and I decided to take one child each to our God-given assignments. I went with our youngest child, the baby boy, headed for New

Wine Church, while my husband went on to preach at our local church, taking our young daughter with him. I arrived promptly at the church before the service was to begin and was warmly welcomed by the church ushers. They took our young son to the children's nursery, and I went into the main hall to join the morning worship service.

The program began by welcoming the congregation, followed with opening prayers, after which the praise and worship team led the congregation in songs. It was soon time for my gospel solo, after which the special guest would preach. Before the service began, I had given a member of the sound department the accompanying music for my song on an audio cassette (this was back in the day before CDs and streaming). I got up to sing, waiting for my accompanying music track to begin. On this occasion, the only time that I can recall during my many visits to the New Wine Church, the sound and music systems suddenly all stopped working. With a packed house and a well-known special guest speaker at his seat waiting, the highly organized New Wine ministers took swift action to correct the mishap. I quietly prayed and waited at the altar in front.

A few minutes later, the issue was resolved, my music began to play, and I completed my song, albeit a bit flustered. After the service, I was introduced to and greeted the special guest, Pastor Tunde Bakare. I chatted briefly with him and apologized for not being able to give my best rendition of the song due to the interruption. He greeted me warmly, and I scheduled an appointment to meet with him a few days later at the London residence where he was staying with his family before his return home to Lagos.

I did not fully realize it at the time, but I was later to find out what a rare and very special privilege this was. There was usually a long waiting list of people trying to obtain a few minutes audience with him, so being granted one so effortlessly had to be God. At our meeting, I shared with him what the Lord had been doing in my life and the new album I was in the process of completing and releasing. The words he spoke next would be another of God's precious faith lessons to me. To paraphrase, he said that, during the incident of the sound recording failure at the church, he had carefully observed my spontaneous reaction and attitude to the interruption. Giving all the credit to God, he shared that there was no shortage of great artists for his ministry in Nigeria. However, he stated that many artists, even Christian ones, can be rude, impatient, and temperamental when things do not run smoothly. The thing that affected him most about me on the day was not just my singing, but my peaceful, calm reaction to the disruption. Only God could have arranged such an unusual way for Christ's character to be on display! God knew that for this great man, who already had access to some of the greatest talents available, to trust and assist me, he would need more than a singing performance.

Talent, training, and knowledge are essential, necessary, and very important, but these are not all we need to access God's purpose and destinies for our lives. It was the fruit of Christ in the heart, not only in my performance, that would prove crucial. Sometimes we think valuable opportunities belong only to the talented people in life, those with the greatest skills. However, God talks about motive and character more than talent. When it comes to God's way of promoting a person, character is what He evaluates, and it is what defines us. God wants us to walk in His footsteps and follow his example of good character. If we are truly living lives of faith, we must also strive to build good Christian character. The word of God instructs us:

> For this very reason, make every effort to supplement your faith with virtue, and virtue with knowledge, and knowledge with self-control, and self-control with steadfastness, and steadfastness with godliness, and godliness with brotherly affection, and brotherly affection with love. (2 Peter 1:5–7, ESV)

> But the fruit of the Spirit is love, joy, peace, patience, kindness, goodness, faithfulness,

gentleness, self-control; against such things there is no law. (Galatians 5:22–23, NIV)

And we know that God causes everything to work together for the good of those who love God and are called according to his purpose for them. (Romans 8:28, NLT)

I'm not certain if this were his own original words, but I once heard a precious servant of Christ say "deepen your ministry first, then God will widen it." In other words, if we seek God's character and righteousness within ourselves first, then all other blessings will be added to us. "But seek first his kingdom and his righteousness, and all these things will be given to you as well" (Matthew 6:33, NIV). In the final analysis, when everything is said and done, for God to open great doors and greatly work through us, our characters will prove to be more important than our gifts. Based solely on my unrehearsed response to what many others might have considered as the enemy trying to block success, and he may very well have been trying to do just that, it only assisted me to receive yet another miracle from the Lord!

No weapon forged against you will prevail, and you will refute every tongue that accuses you. This is the heritage of the servants of the

LORD, and this is their vindication from me,"
declares the LORD. (Isaiah 54:17, NIV)

Tell the righteous it will be well with them, for
they will enjoy the fruit of their deeds. (Isaiah
3:10, NIV)

No one but you can stop the fulfillment of God's
promises over your life!

The generous and highly influential Pastor Bakare
hosted the successful launch of my first album, *Devotion*," in a week-long celebration during the annual leadership conference that took place from June 1 through 4,
1995, at his church, the Latter Rain Assembly, in Lagos,
Nigeria. The album sold out!

Bakare then introduced me to the famous Nigerian
recording artist-turned-evangelist, Ebenezer Obey. The
Obey family hosted me at their church and on their
television and radio shows, promoting the Lord's work
through their ministry. Their bookstore Decross repackaged and made *Devotion* available for sale and distribution in Nigeria. Wow! One God encounter changes life
forever!

I had been transformed by God from a career in
financial services into becoming a gospel singer, songwriter, and preacher. As an added update, on October 4,
2015, I was again privileged to celebrate more than two
decades of God's amazing grace in a reunion with the

Latter Rain Assembly family in Lagos, as Pastor Tunde Bakare dedicated my latest work, titled *"Amazing Grace,"* at the church. A few words from this great hymn written by John Newton are as follows.

> Amazing grace how sweet the sound,
> That saved a wretch like me
> I once was lost but now I am found,
> I was blind but now I see.

Chapter Twelve

1995, God's Just Getting Started

In the mid- to late-1990s, as my new calling began to take shape, I spent much of my time traveling, while we continued to build our family. Praise God! God was not even close to completing the work of major transformation that he had begun in my life during the amazing year of 1995. While seeking God through prayer and fasting in preparation for a ministry invitation, I had decided to consecrate a few days to Him. I was to break my fast on the final day at 6 p.m. but suddenly began to feel extremely hungry and unusually faint and tired early on the final day. Wanting to break earlier than the scheduled time, I was almost ready to quit when I felt the Lord's encouragement cheering me on. He also impressed very strongly on my spirit that He would release a very special blessing to me that day if I did not quit. I was still contemplating quitting and had almost succumbed to temptation, ready to give in to my weakness, when the phone rang. I had suddenly received a phone call from a Christian friend who proceeded to chat with me, and before I knew it, the official time for me to break the fast was up! God surely is a wonderful helper and an expert at strengthening the weary. We chatted for so long that I forgot the time and how exhausted I was. Another of His promises states,

> He gives strength to the weary and increases the power of the weak. (Isaiah 40:29, NIV)

> I will refresh the weary and satisfy the faint. (Jeremiah 31:25, NIV)

A few days afterward, God's reward came in a very big way as He had promised. I received an invitation to minister in song at a women's meeting being held at a hotel in London. The special guest speaker was an American missionary living in Scotland. The Lord impressed strongly upon her as I sang that she should invite me to minister in special songs at the women's conference that she annually hosted. I accepted her invitation and attended the event from April 21 to 23, 1995, in Scotland, accompanied by the women's fellowship leader from my local church. God had, however, meant serious business when He spoke to my heart not to give up my fast that day, as this would turn out to be no ordinary invitation. In attendance at the event was an African American woman of God named Evangelist Christine Liddell, coordinator of one of the largest Christian women's conferences for women of color in the United States at that time, the EC Reems Women's International Conference (this was before Woman Thou Art Loosed and Megafest). This yearly event, named after its founder Bishop Ernestine Cleveland Reems, was again about to become a major turning point in my life and our family's lives.

While I had ministered during the conference, the Lord again invaded the room. His tangible presence was so powerfully manifested that the American lady evangelist, Christine Liddell, felt prompted during that three-day event to invite me to a major women's conference. It was the shortest of notices and scheduled to take place the following month, May 17 to 20, 1995, in Washington, DC. With just a few days left to obtain visas, arrange childcare, and pack, I finally found myself at the venue for the event, the Sheraton Hotel ballroom in Washington, DC, only a short distance from the White House!

The event was attended by the most recognized and prolific preachers in the nation. Bishop Reems was a gracious and generous host. I was especially privileged to join her, Evangelist Liddell, and a small company of ladies in the very early morning prayers each day of the almost week-long event, seeking God's heart for all the attendees. After the evening services, I joined her other special guests in her personal suite to enjoy fellowship with and be encouraged by many well-respected and renowned Christian leaders of the time.

However, the Lord still had more surprises in store for me. Despite some of the most gifted and famous American gospel artists of our time being Bishop E. C. Reems's spiritual sons and daughters (her late father Bishop Cleveland had been a spiritual mentor to many of our well-known and beloved gospel artists), I was granted the honor of ministering as the solo artist before their special guest speaker came up on stage to speak. Backed by the largest choir I'd been privileged to work with up until that point, I sang and prepared the atmosphere to welcome and usher in God's presence. That special servant of God was none other than Bishop T. D. Jakes, now a famous preacher all over the globe.

God's divine set ups did not at all end there! He was actually only just getting started. On one of the afternoon break times during the conference, while I was getting ready to take a nap before the big evening service, one of my assigned protocol hostesses suddenly called for me. "There is somebody I'd like you to meet," she said, so I quickly got dressed and followed her to the hotel ballroom. "This is Evangelist Sandra Crouch, twin sister of the famed songwriter and gospel artist Andrae Crouch." This time I was now familiar with the name, having previously sung his song at the RCCG event and just recently read about his newest release, a gospel album titled *Mercy*. This legendary gospel music great, whose name was written at the end of many of our worship songs, had worked with every famous artist on earth.

His songs have been recorded by everyone from Elvis Presley to Paul Simon, and he has worked as a producer and arranger with many of music's top artists, including Michael Jackson, Madonna, Quincy Jones, Diana Ross, and Elton John. Andrae can also be heard on Michael Jackson's hit singles "Man in the Mirror," "Keep the Faith," "Will You Be There," and "Earth Song." This God-ordained encounter with evangelist Sandra Crouch would result in a friendship over many years with her and her "twin" the generous, humble, loving, accessible, Grammy-award-winning, star-on-Hollywood-walk-of-fame, brother-in-the-Lord, Pastor Andrae Crouch. Over the years I was privileged to minister for and prophesy over them both on many occasions at the local church they both pastored. The church, originally founded by their parents, was the New Christ Memorial Church, in Pacoima, California. I was also blessed to share the word with him backstage at the Trinity Broadcasting Network's television station studios in Tustin, California, before he would go on their live "Praise the Lord" program, accompanied by a mutual friend, Sister Evelyn. Evangelist Sandra Crouch a few years later also invited me to attend her official ordination and preservice reception ceremony for her new position as co-pastor at their church. At that event, I was privileged to meet the special speaker for the day, author and preacher, the late Doctor Myles Monroe.

I am today still in awe of God for the many great privileges and amazing encounters, experiences, and memories I will forever cherish. Upon Pastor Andrae's passing in January 2015, his twin sister, Pastor Sandra Crouch, again granted me the honor of VIP seating alongside friends of many years to celebrate his life at the West Angeles Cathedral in Los Angeles, California. The president of the United States released the following statement to honor Pastor Andrae:

> Michelle and I were saddened to learn of the passing of music legend Pastor Andrae Crouch. Pastor Crouch grew up the son of a minister in California and discovered at a young age that he was blessed with extraordinary musical talent which would lead to an iconic career that spanned over fifty years. As a leading pioneer of contemporary gospel music, the soulful classics that Pastor Crouch created over the years have uplifted the hearts and minds of several generations and his timeless influence continues to be felt in not only gospel but a variety of music genres. We are grateful that his music and spirit will continue to live on for years to come and our thoughts and prayers are with his family, friends, and fans during this time. —President Barack Obama

Chapter Thirteen

AUDACIOUS FAITH
MOVE TO AMERICA

In 1995, God's prophetic destiny for our lives suddenly exploded and unfolded all at once! Before I knew it, I was all over the map; first attending the women's conference in Scotland in April, followed by the Washington, DC, invitation in May, swiftly followed by the journey in June to present my first album, *Devotion*, at the Latter Rain Assembly in Lagos, Nigeria. Looking back on that period now, this was clearly God's year of undeniable elevation for us. After my return from the journeys to Washington, DC, and Nigeria in June, it became clear to us that we must *now* say *yes* to God's call to North America! He had opened this mighty door for us that no man can shut, and we had no choice but to walk through it.

> I know your deeds. See, I have placed before you an open door that no one can shut. I know that you have little strength, yet you have kept my word and have not denied my name. (Revelation 3:8, NIV)

The Holy Spirit had now created a new sense of urgency in our spirits. Knowing that being out of the will of God is a place you never want to be, as it is a place that God cannot go with you, we finally committed to His plan. "If anyone, then, knows the good they ought to do and doesn't do it, it is sin for them" (James 4:17, NIV). Next we needed to know exactly which of the fifty states that make up the huge United States of America God had in mind for us to go. This was way too big for our finite minds. After many, many prayers and multiple signs and confirmations from the Lord, He led us to finally solve the puzzle and recognize that it was the great state of California.

It was precisely Southern California. This did not seem like great news to us at the time when we found out how expensive California was. Lord, we are going there by faith? How? Nonetheless, in full obedience, we offered the rest of our lives to God and headed for the new territory He had called us to. Initiated and led by the Lord, our permanent relocation to the United States had to be brought to full manifestation and completion by Him. Knowing that we could not possibly fulfill or fund such an impossibly large venture, God's word that He was the provider became even more alive and real to us than ever before. We decided to give up our entire lives and net worth as *seed*, trusting Him for *everything*.

"For I know the plans I have for you," declares the LORD, "plans to prosper you and not to harm you, plans to give you hope and a future." (Jeremiah 29:11, NIV)

And everyone who has left houses or brothers or sisters or father or mother or wife or children or fields for my sake will receive a hundred times as much and will inherit eternal life. (Matthew 19:29, NIV)

But seek first his kingdom and his righteousness, and all these things will be given to you as well. (Matthew 6:33, NIV)

Sowing almost everything we owned to various Christian ministries, organizations, family members, and friends, I finally left England for the United States with our very young son. The date was August 18, 1995. By His guidance and wisdom, we decided to leave England in teams of two. I would go first with our son and later be joined by my husband and daughter. Jide would stay in England for a few more weeks to complete the handover of our house and wrap up our other affairs. We held on only to the funds needed for our airline tickets and some pocket change we had received as gifts from two Christian couples. Taking our greatest leap of faith ever, we leapt by faith over the mighty chasm of the unknown into God's perfect plan.

This final audacious step of faith would be our response to God, and we were not looking back. We believed that because our move was wholly and solely in obedience to God, He would meet us on the other side, multiplying all our precious seeds into a bountiful harvest of souls for His kingdom. My plan was to first fly to San Francisco, which is in the northern part of California, and then on to our final destination in Southern California.

The way God reveals himself in our most trying and stressful moments is truly precious and wonderful. He calms our fears and wipes our tears. I state this because I must testify to His devoted care as a parent to His children. Our son, who was just under two years old at the time, almost always insisted on being carried around by my husband. They were extremely close, and if anyone else even so much as blinked at him he would cry. No one else was allowed to get too close or was popular with him. The only other two people allowed to come close to him occasionally to feed or play with him, and only if his father was unavailable, were his sister and me. All other times, he wanted to be lifted up and carried in his father's strong arms. This arrangement was fine with me as I could do with the break after having carried him for over nine months and then delivered him.

However, this baby habit that we all used to laugh about, and until now had not been a problem, would add to my stress level as the departure date drew closer. We now realized that it could be a big problem when it was time to take him from his dad at the airport.

The uncertainty of everything that lay ahead, except for God's word, was already overwhelming for us both. My husband was trying to hide his concern about our son and me, leaving without him to care for us, and I was just out of it trying to focus only on God's word and not think negatively. In those circumstances, the very thought of having to wrench an extremely upset baby from my husband's arms and pacify him throughout the eleven-hour flight was too much for me to add to my already-full plate. However, our God is faithful and kind and truly cares about even the smallest details of our lives. His supernatural and mighty acts are not just for great occasions, such as parting the Red Sea, but also for separating very clingy and cranky toddlers from their weary parents!

The day we were to leave for San Francisco arrived, and as we drove to Heathrow airport as a family, we all dreaded the moment of their separation and quietly prayed. We had no strength left to spare for this little drama that my son would view as a major trauma in his young mind. But on this one occasion— and this is the only occasion on which this had ever happened— we watched, stunned, as a move of God again unfolded before our eyes. Our son, without a thought or any struggle, happily relinquished himself from his father's arms, let go of his dad's hands, and quietly placed his little hands in mine as we walked to board our flight. God will surely take care of you.

He was the happiest and quietest I had ever seen him throughout the entire flight. Everyone around commented on what a cooperative and happy son I had, and I knew whom all the credit should go to. He remained that way until we landed and throughout our entire stay in Northern California and later on in Minnesota, where we were reunited with his dad and sister. The faith lessons here are simple and best summarized by the following scriptures. We are not to allow stress and weariness to become a yoke, clouding our expectations even in the smallest areas of our lives. God's promises are powerful, awesome, and true!

> Come to me, all you who are weary and burdened, and I will give you rest. Take my yoke upon you and learn from me, for I am gentle and humble in heart, and you will find rest for your souls. (Matthew 11:28–29, NIV)

> I am leaving you with a gift—peace of mind and heart. And the peace I give is a gift the world cannot give. So don't be troubled or afraid. (John 14:27, NIV)

When we all finally resettled at our new Southern California residence, he returned to his usual personality, confirming that this indeed had been entirely God's doing. After arriving in the United States, I waited at the San Francisco airport with my toddler son for the Christian lady and her family who were to meet us at the airport and host us for a few days. This arrangement had been agreed on with them before leaving England. They never showed, so I placed a call and caught up with the wonderful Evangelist Christine Liddell just before she left the office for the day, who immediately sent someone to pick up my son and me. We spent the first night at her place. Praise God; we had arrived safely on the other side!

The next day I proceeded with our son to the home of a prayer intercessor I had met at the Scottish conference. Trust God to have worked things together for good. Because the other lady had reneged on her promise to host us for a few days, I ended up staying instead at the home of a prayer warrior, the perfect location for prayer support and covering for such a supernatural venture. I guess that the other lady must have suddenly got cold feet about walking by faith. However, God *never* fails!

> So be strong and courageous! Do not be afraid
> and do not panic before them. For the LORD
> your God will personally go ahead of you. He

will neither fail you nor abandon you. (Deuteronomy 31:6, NLT)

Don't be afraid, for I am with you. Don't be dis-
couraged, for I am your God. I will strengthen
you and help you. I will hold you up with my
victorious right hand. (Isaiah 41:10, NLT)

My son and I stayed a few weeks with the intercessor and her family in Northern California, sharing with
their family from whatever love gifts the Lord blessed
us with. I then headed with our son to Minnesota to
preach at a revival by invitation from some pastors there.
All the praises must again go to our awesome and faithful God! He provided all the necessary funds, and my
husband and daughter finally joined us in Minnesota
for the weeklong conference. It was a joyous reunion.
We had all made it through to the other side, arriving
together safely in our place of divine appointment, the
United States of America. God had brought all of us
over victoriously.

After the conference we decided that my husband
would stay and rest for a few more days in Minnesota
with the children. I went ahead to prepare a home for
all of us in Southern California. Making our travel
arrangements with the love gifts received from the ministries I had been privileged to serve, my journey to our
new, God-appointed place in Southern California was

the most frightening one I've ever undertaken. As I said goodbye to my husband and children at the airport in Minnesota, I was suddenly attacked by great fear. There were no more spiritual, emotional, or financial crutches as I boarded the plane to California. My husband would not be on the flight with me, or we could have encouraged and reminded one other of God's word and promises. Our young children were also not present, which would have helped pull me together in a show of courage for their sakes. I was now left, bare-knuckled, alone with God! "So Jacob was left alone" (Genesis 32:24, NIV).

The full weight and realization of what we had done by leaving our secure, familiar, and comfortable lives in England slowly, clearly, and heavily dawned upon me. Alone, I was headed to the vast new area of Southern California, a place we had no knowledge of and where we knew not one soul. I had almost completely given in to all the fear and trepidation of the great unknown when the Holy Spirit came to my aid. He began to softly and vividly remind me of the many scriptures, prophetic encounters, and multitudes of confirmations through which He had led us to this point. As the Lord gently calmed my spirit, I began to force myself to recall, recount, and repeat many scriptures throughout the entire flight.

> But all who listen to me will live in peace, untroubled by fear of harm. (Proverbs 1:33, NIV)

The LORD is my shepherd, I lack nothing.
(Psalm 23:1, NIV)

And my God will meet all your needs according
to the riches of his glory in Christ Jesus. (Philippians 4:19, NIV)

Fear the LORD, you his holy people, for those
who fear him lack nothing. (Psalm 34:9, NIV)

But he brought his people out like a flock; he
led them like sheep through the wilderness.
(Psalm 78:52, NIV)

He will not let your foot slip—he who watches
over you will not slumber. (Psalm 121:3, NIV)

This is a big key to faith when our minds are
swamped by negativity, such as depression, guilt, shame,
fear, loss, addiction, isolation, and so on. Whether it's
personal or we are trying to assist those who are temporarily unable to help themselves, we must lay hold of
God's word. Grasp in the darkness of your mind for the
light of God's word, the scriptures. The power to escape
from darkness into light is within them. This is really and
truly the only effective way out. Whether we are alone in
a hospital, receiving treatment for a life-threatening ill-
ness, or find ourselves in a very dark and dreadful place,

we must run to God, not from Him. As the airplane got close to landing, I began to see what seemed like a sea of little lights below. They represented the many Southern Californian homes and a multitude of strangers. The fears arose up again and almost completely engulfed me, but many more scriptures rushed to my aid, calming and reassuring me to focus on God and not on our circumstances. We had given up our secure lives for what might look to others as irresponsible uncertainty. We now owned no front door keys to a house, keys to a car, or any other keys; it appeared that we now owned *nothing*. At this point, I had neglected another of God's faith principles and the very first scripture promise I had received from Him.

> The earth is the LORD's, and everything in it. The world and all its people belong to him. (Psalm 24:1, NLT).

> After all, we brought nothing with us when we came into the world, and we can't take anything with us when we leave it. (1 Timothy 6:7, NLT)

We really had always owned nothing and were only stewards of the possessions and earthly blessings that God had kindly allowed us to have. We will take none of these things with us when we leave.

Other thoughts also swiftly raced through my mind and with them the reminder of the fact that there were no longer any family members, friends, intercessors, evangelists, pastors, companies, or any other people waiting for us on the other side. Every single one of those "sea of lights" belonged to a stranger. I could draw strength only from God's word. This was the very first time in my walk of faith that I could truly say there was *no thing* left to attach my life and faith to, or from which I could draw reassurance. My education, previous experiences, finances, work experience, and network of family, church, friends, and so forth were not going to help me in this awesome moment of great transition.

My old life with all its crutches (although I had not previously identified them as such) no longer existed. We do not realize how much of our security we have rooted and connected to our families; where we live, grow, work, and find fellowship; and where loved ones, family, and friends are all around us. Without realizing it, we may draw more strength and security from those ties than from our relationship with God. Many Christians, within the comfort of our faith communities and familiar everyday surroundings, are lulled into believing and thinking that we really and fully *trust* God for all our needs. We often say to ourselves and others that we depend on God and have no doubt that He is our source and provider.

However, in those very rare moments when the familiar—that is, people, surroundings, good health, and other normal life structures—are temporarily affected or removed, we may be surprised to fully experience how much we really know, believe, and depend on God and His word alone. When all these things are stripped away from us, we may gain an occasional rare glimpse into how much of our security and identity are rooted in them instead of in God.

Chapter Fourteen

Arriving in a Strange Land

My arrival in Southern California was met by many manifestations of God's supernatural acts. God, in His mercy, had faithfully accompanied, led, and met me on the other side as He had promised. Without knowing a soul when I arrived, and with no credit history, income, or even a social security number, I was blessed with God's favor to secure a very beautiful two-bedroom apartment, with sparkling swimming pools for our use, located in a secure, gated community in Costa Mesa, California. This would be our very first home in the area. My family joined me there a few days later. We had given up all our old keys in England for our house, car, and so on, and God had given us brand *new* keys. The God of the impossible again showed up as He had promised.

> Jesus looked at them and said, "With man this is impossible, but with God all things are possible." (Matthew 19:26, NIV)

Behold, I am the LORD, the God of all flesh. Is anything too hard for me? (Jeremiah 32:27, ESV)

Is anything too hard for the LORD? I will return to you at the appointed time next year, and Sarah will have a son. (Genesis 18:14, NIV)

One of the many miracles was when I met a young stockbroker, originally from Liberia, by the name of George. It was during a visit to a church that happened to be within walking distance from our new apartment. California is the third-largest state in America by area and the largest by population. With a population of over thirty-eight million people and no underground or rail system, a car is almost a necessity. At some point during the church service, we were all asked to turn and greet the people around us. After saying my hellos to the people on either side of me, I turned to greet the people in the row behind me, including a young man sitting right behind my chair.

God had arranged everything in his usual, amazingly precise style. That young man could have been seated anywhere in the five hundred or so congregation meeting space. We chatted briefly, and he introduced himself as George. I was to find out later that he had never attended that church before and was just visiting that day on an invitation from his neighbor. He asked me what I was doing in California, and I tried to explain "walking by faith" to him. Whatever he understood me to have said, God moved upon his heart, and he decided to fully furnish our new place with some top-of-the-line furniture. I immediately recalled sowing all our beautiful furniture in England along with my left-over wedding gifts and was just in awe of God's principle of sowing and reaping. He had again fulfilled His promise to us, restoring so rapidly and abundantly much more than we had sown.

> And everyone who has left houses or brothers or sisters or father or mother or wife or children or fields for my sake will receive a hundred times as much and will inherit eternal life. (Matthew 19:29, NIV)

George also very kindly volunteered to pick my husband and our children up from the airport when they arrived from Minnesota. Afterward, he gave us all a tour of the area, sharing many valuable pieces of information with us.

The miracles continued as many Christians in the area begin to hear of our supernatural move to California. The miracles of God's provision, manifestations of His great power, and His call upon our lives seemed endless. One of the first people to hear of us was a Nigerian pastor by the name of Tony. He introduced us to a

Christian couple living in Garden Grove, California. This couple, upon hearing of our amazing God encounters, immediately arranged for us to meet their senior pastors, Doctors Ric and Renee Durfield. The name of their church was Christ Temple Church in Pomona, California, later renamed Eagle Heights Community Church after they moved their congregation to Chino, California. Dr. Durfield, PhD, CFL, was, until his retirement, a professor of theology at Azusa Pacific University, in Azusa, California. The Durfields are the founders of two successful and highly recognized ministries. In addition to having authored several books, they have contributed to such publications as *Focus on the Family* (April 1990) and *Charisma* (March 1992). Meeting them was a great honor from the Lord.

Again, this was solely orchestrated by God. The Durfields immediately took us under their wings and provided great support. With their assistance, we were able to complete all of the necessary paperwork to register and preach as ordained clergy in the United States. One of the churches in Minnesota had also agreed to sponsor and file for the extension and completion of the needed paperwork to finalize our permanent immigration status. Pastors Ric and Renee opened the doors of their church and pulpit to us, embracing and encouraging God's call upon our lives. From our arrival and for many years later, I was privileged to receive invitations to preach and sing at their church and special events.

The next memorable encounter was with the late Pastor Eddie Rodriguez, senior pastor of On Fire Ministries in Anaheim, California, a Foursquare church. He was a wonderful man of God whose ministry operated men's homes, which were a form of rehabilitation and residential center to help drug addicts and alcoholics in their fight to stay clean and regain sobriety. Someone had invited me to visit his church and offered to pick me up and take me back home after the service. We arrived at the church, and I sat toward the back in what was a fairly large congregation. There is no natural explanation for what happened next, except to recognize and acknowledge the undeniable hand of our God. During the worship service, I joined in with the many voices in praise as we sang songs of adoration to God. My eyes were closed and my focus was entirely on worshipping God with all my heart. I noticed nothing of any other activities that may have been going on around me. I was a visitor at the church and knew no one in the congregation, except the person who had invited me to the service.

Immediately after the service, the senior pastor, whose name I later learned was Pastor Eddie Rodriguez, sent someone to get me from the back row where I was seated. I wondered why and quietly followed the usher to Pastor Eddie's office. A few of his pastors from other branches were sitting around him and he invited me to sit down. He then asked who I was and how I had come to the service that day. I proceeded to share a very brief version of our testimony with him. He listened with rapt attention. After I finished speaking, he shared with me that as I worshipped during the service, he had noticed a radiance around where I had been standing with my hands uplifted. The radiance grew, and he sensed a strong presence of the Holy Spirit upon me. He had pastored the church for many years and had never seen me before, so he wanted to find out who I was. After he heard the testimony, he asked me to bring my husband and family for a service so he could meet them.

When I got home I shared all that had just taken place with my husband, and we were again picked up for the next service at the Anaheim church. After the service, I introduced my family to Pastor Eddie, and he repeated to my husband the account of what he had experienced during my last visit to the church. Again, the Lord had prepared the way in his own very wonderful style.

Pastor Eddie stated that he believed the Lord wanted him to be a blessing to us and he opened the doors of the ministry and all its branches to us. He also personally spoke to many of his pastors, recommending our ministry to them. Due to the high regard all the pastors had for him, many invitations to sing and preach followed. More doors to minister in Southern California's cities begin to open: Los Angeles, Anaheim, Fontana, Barstow, San Bernadino, Whittier, and many more. As word of our ministry spread, I was invited to preach and minister in all over Southern California. Invitations to minister in other states were also soon received as the snowball of God's divine network continued to grow.

A lady by the name of Evelyn, originally from the Central African state now known as the Democratic Republic of the Congo, also heard about our story and called. We had said yes to her request to visit us, and it turned out to be another extraordinary encounter. The odds of what happened next can again only be attributed to God. During my conversation with her, I happened to share the account of my extraordinary journey to Washington, DC, and my meeting with an evangelist, Sandra Crouch, earlier that year. Sister Evelyn looked astounded, and I wondered what the expression on her face could possibly mean. It turned out that she was a very close family friend of many years with the Crouch family, and she immediately called Sister Sandra on the phone, reconnecting me with her. I had thought nothing of it when the Lord introduced us in Washington, DC. The place had been jam-packed with many very well-known Christian personalities, and I had not thought at the time to ask Evangelist Sandra what state she resided in.

I had lived in England at the time, and really wasn't expecting to ever see her again. Due to my cave-like mentality, I was also not yet aware of the fame of my new friend. Perhaps I never would have fully realized it but for the intervention of our Heavenly Father. I also may never have noticed that I was now within driving distance of Pastors Andrae and Sandra Crouch. Wow!

As soon as Evangelist Sandra found out that I was now local to her in Southern California and no longer in England, she immediately sent me invitations to preach and minister at their new church in Pacoima. They had just recently taken over after the passing of their father and older brother, and I was privileged to be a blessing to them and the congregation. What are the statistical odds of all these perfectly synchronized events taking place? I have only one answer that makes sense: God!

The Crouches asked me over to their church to minister often, and also hosted an aptly titled "Prophetic Explosion" conference. I was privileged to be one of their four keynote speakers. As I shared earlier, our friendship would continue until Pastor Andrae's passing in January 2015. I look forward to the reunions when we all get to heaven. I am privileged to still call Pastor Sandra my friend.

Chapter Fifteen

TROUBLE

No work of God goes unchallenged, and we were about to experience a series of major attacks as we continued to settle down in California. Having filled out and filed all the necessary paperwork to the immigration and naturalization department through the Minnesota church, we were patiently awaiting their response and the completion of our permanent immigration status. After almost a year of repeated phone calls to the Minnesota ministry that yielded no updates on the status of our application, we took matters into our own hands. Sometime during the year 1996, we finally decided to call the INS directly to inquire about our pending application. What we found out next was bad news, and the first major disappointment since our arrival.

The INS proceeded to inform us that they had requested some additional information from our sponsors quite a while back, and had sent the church some necessary forms for us to fill out and return. The forms had to be completed and returned to the INS by the given deadline stated in their accompanying letter to the church. In an attempt to hinder God's work, the spirit of "cold feet" had apparently struck again. The church confirmed receipt of the INS request but, for reasons best known only to them, had changed their minds about completing the process. They ignored the official request and had abandoned our application without ever notifying us. Had they simply informed us of their change of heart in a timely manner, we could have promptly replaced them with new sponsors from our Southern Californian contacts.

This was a very significant blow that would take over a decade of our lives to resolve and rectify. Because the fault on this occasion was not with the INS, and they had not received a response to their request by the deadline, our application was denied. Shocked to suddenly discover that our status and future had been placed in great jeopardy by this irresponsible act, we turned to the only true friend we knew we had, Jesus.

Unable to take up any employment positions due to the incomplete paperwork, any hope of secular work to support our ministry efforts was now temporarily impossible. This, we would soon discover, was only the beginning of our woes during 1996. Only a year after giving up our all to go after God's will and purpose, it appeared that we were losing far more than we had anticipated. However, God's word reminded us of His promises and what our faith response should be.

Because he has loved Me, therefore I will deliver him; I will set him securely on high, because he has known My name. "He will call upon Me, and I will answer him; I will be with him in trouble; I will rescue him and honor him. With a long life I will satisfy him and let him see My salvation. (Psalm 91:14–16, NASB)

I have told you these things, so that in me you may have peace. In this world you will have trouble. But take heart! I have overcome the world. (John 16:33, NIV)

For our struggle is not against flesh and blood, but against the rulers, against the powers, against the world forces of this darkness, against the spiritual forces of wickedness in the heavenly places. Therefore, take up the full armor of God, so that you will be able to resist in the evil day, and having done everything, to stand firm. (Ephesians 6:12, NASB)

We made the decision to forgive the senior pastors and others involved in this debacle, based on an act of our will, choosing not to dwell on the great difficulty their actions had placed us and our young children in. This did not come easily, but we knew that for us to receive God's best, we had to let go of all of our anger.

Therefore I say to you, all things for which you pray and ask, believe that you have received them, and they will be granted you. Whenever you stand praying, forgive, if you have anything against anyone, so that your Father who is in heaven will also forgive you your transgressions. (Mark 11:24–25, NASB)

Ask, and it will be given to you; seek, and you will find; knock, and it will be opened to you. (Matthew 7:7, NASB)

I did not know at that point how important these scriptures would later be to me. I would need these words again in a few months in order to forgive a far greater crime. The principle of faith known as forgiveness would be my road map out of an extremely deep pit that lay just ahead.

While wondering what to do to resolve our immigration dilemma, many people advised us to just return to England. Some of our family members in England also strongly desired our return. We, however, could not go back on God's clear word to us and deny all that we knew He had done to get us thus far. All doors for now appeared to be closed on our ability to obtain the correct paperwork. Being British citizens the obvious, natural, and easiest solution would have been to return to England, but this was not even close to being an option. We knew from all the principles of faith that God had taught us that going back on His clearly revealed and confirmed word to us would be out of His will.

> You are my friends if you do what I command you. (John 15:14, ESV)

> Samuel said, "Has the LORD as much delight in burnt offerings and sacrifices as in obeying the voice of the LORD? Behold, to obey is better than sacrifice, And to heed than the fat of rams. For rebellion is as the sin of divination, and insubordination is as iniquity and idolatry. Because you have rejected the word of the LORD, He has also rejected you from being king." (1 Samuel 15:22–23, NASB)

> "For I did not speak to your fathers, or command them in the day that I brought them out of the land of Egypt, concerning burnt offerings and sacrifices. But this is what I commanded them, saying, 'Obey My voice, and I will be your God, and you will be My people; and you will walk in all the way which I command you, that it may be well with you.'" (Jeremiah 7:22–23, NASB)

Laboring in prayer as we pondered over what to do next, we waited on the Lord. His answer came, first

through two complete strangers, and then a third witness, a pastor whom we knew and trusted.

We had received an invitation from the Christ
Temple Church in Pomona to attend what I recall to be
a celebration of their church's anniversary. During this
special event in 1996, something similar to what had
initiated our move to the United States from England
occurred. The special guest speaker, a man we had never
heard of or met before, Pastor David Ireland from New
Jersey, begin to prophesy from the pulpit right after fin-
ishing his sermon. He suddenly singled my husband and
me out from the three hundred or so people in the congregation. Asking us to stand up, he spoke words over us.
I share some of the most relevant words as they flowed
out from him: "I see boxes packed. I see boxes packed,
and you are in transition. The Lord says, 'Unpack your
boxes. I am going to move regarding every governmental issue in your lives and plant you right where you are.'
. . . There is a call on you and an apostolic grace on your
lives." He then turned to me and said, "My daughter,
you are one who says, 'Not me, not me, not me,' but
the Lord has called you! 'Don't you remember the many
visions I have given you? The many dreams I have shown
you?' God has given you a heart for children. Children
who are cast aside by society. . . . You are called to be a
prophetess and preacher in God's house."

Wow! Everyone who knew about our immigration story and the prophetic nature of my ministry was

amazed at his accuracy. That was quite the supernatural answer.

Someone else had made a last-minute invitation to me during this same period to meet and visit with a bishop from Uganda, who was flying back home on that same day. We met him in the lobby of the inn from which he had just checked out. He had never seen me before or since the day he spoke the following words: "I was praying this morning before you came, and the Lord clearly spoke to me about someone coming to see me. He said this person [I] had not at all desired to move to America. Many want to move here but not you. But God wants you here; He wants you to continue here with His work." I was again astounded!

Finally a trusted and experienced pastor and mentor of ours became the third witness. He confirmed what the other two strangers had spoken, in more or less the same words. Then he shared a scripture the Lord had laid on his heart for us: **For God is not unjust so as to overlook your work and the love that you have shown for his name in serving the saints, as you still do** (Hebrews 6:10, ESV).

Well, all these witnesses fulfilled yet another scripture: "This will be my third visit to you. Every matter must be established by the testimony of two or three witnesses" (2 Corinthians 13:1, NIV). Case closed! We would never look back again. There was, however, a much more vicious attack from the enemy ahead, another effort to completely stop our family's momentum in God. Right in the midst of all the unsettling immigration and other challenges, the worst news came.

Chapter Sixteen

DEVASTATING NEWS

On a bright Californian Sunday morning in December of that same year, 1996, right in the midst of all our immigration disputes, I suddenly received an early phone call. One of my uncles was on the other end of the call and said, "Your father has been assassinated." My world naturally stopped. I screamed! And I instantly recalled a very supernatural experience I had overnight that had only been interrupted by the loud ringing of the telephone in the morning, waking me up to the terrible news. The many tears would come later, accompanied by all of the agonies of laying a dearly beloved one to rest.

I immediately tried to find out where my mother was, and was informed that she had been rushed back from a week-long Christian conference she had been attending and was now at her pastor's house. I lost all reasoning for a while when no one seemed to have the pastor's home phone number. I called every minister I thought might know his number. It took a few hours before I finally reached and got to speak to my mom in Nigeria. Dad's death is still a bit of a mystery, but a few details later emerged.

Due to his extensive involvement in acquiring land for the use of various Christian organizations, he had previously been targeted and threatened by people with connections to Islamic extremism. It is believed that some of the land he had helped to purchase may have been of interest to people connected with the Islamic faith for their own intended use. Unknown gunmen were sent to carry out their threats by executing him. This was and still is a very rare occurrence in the southern part of Nigeria, as many faiths and ethnic groups had dwelt side by side peacefully for many generations, and still do so. This was also long before the emergence of the Boko Haram terrorist group, which still largely operates in the northern part of Nigeria. This violent trend against Christians was not at all taken seriously in those very early days as such incidents had never happened before. His death made front-page news in the Nigerian national *Daily Sketch Newspaper* of Tuesday, December 10, 1996.

Our grief was unquantifiable as we very slowly came to terms with the tragedy. All four of us, his children, were later given letters he had handwritten to each one of us that had been found around him. Mine was dated December 5, 1996. He had just finished writing the very last of the letters earlier on that fateful morning when the attackers called him to our front porch and fatally shot him. I still have my dad's final letter to me carefully put away in pristine condition among my treasured things. In it, he had thanked us for the Christmas card we had sent to them that year and prayed blessings upon us for the New Year. He had also expressed his deep gratitude to me for supporting my siblings during all the earlier tribulations and trials the family went through. How kind God was to let Dad's final words to us be recorded in his own handwriting while we were all so far away. Being the oldest child, the primary responsibility of strengthening our heartbroken mother and supporting my siblings again fell on me.

How I was able to travel to Nigeria and fulfill all my duties toward his burial in the light of our uncompleted immigration papers, remains one of God's mightiest displays of His power. I am unable to share the details of this huge miracle with you as many would simply find it too hard to believe. I will only testify to the fact that God's power is real, His grace is unsurmountable, and I have experienced his mighty acts. By this great grace, I went to Nigeria for the burial and returned safely back to my family in California.

Many wonderful people carried us through this extremely dark period in every way possible. Collectively shocked and overwhelmed as a family, we could not "walk." After moving my mom from her pastor's house, the Akinyele family took her temporarily into their home, caring for her and the family as we all traveled to Nigeria from England, North America, and many other places. Chief T. A. Akinyele had been the Director of

Budget and Special Adviser on Budget Affairs to former Nigerian President Shehu Shagari from 1979–1983. He and his family were close friends of my parents, and they entertained the many people who daily stopped by or called to offer support and condolences.

> Can anything ever separate us from Christ's love? Does it mean he no longer loves us if we have trouble or calamity, or are persecuted, or hungry, or destitute, or in danger, or threatened with death? (Romans 8:35, NIV)

> We are afflicted in every way, but not crushed; perplexed, but not despairing; persecuted, but not forsaken; struck down, but not destroyed. (2 Corinthians 4:8–9, NIV)

When our mother seemed, at one point, to be completely lost in her grief, I could only think to sing her the words of Micah 7:8 as a worship song. My youngest brother, Big B, and other people present joined in with my singing in an attempt to reach her mind with God's word.

> Rejoice not over me, O my enemy; when I fall, I shall rise; when I sit in darkness, the LORD will be a light to me. (Micah 7:8, ESV)

But we do not want you to be uninformed, brethren, about those who are asleep, so that you will not grieve as do the rest who have no hope. For if we believe that Jesus died and rose again, even so God will bring with Him those who have fallen asleep in Jesus. (1 Thessalonians 4:13–14, NIV)

When all the necessary arrangements for our beloved father following his untimely death were fully completed, he was laid to rest on our family estate. A local poet graced him with the following words to summarize his life.

You served your family with affection.

You served your Church with commitment and openness.

You served your generation with zeal.

You served humanity with concern.

The founder and presiding bishop of his local church, The Christ Life Church, aka Sword of the Spirit Ministries, Bishop Francis Wale Oke, named one of the church's major buildings after our late father, and it still bears his name today: Elder Olu Olarewaju Hall.

I went to the British embassy in Nigeria and obtained a visa for our mother to recuperate for a while in England, after which she subsequently traveled to South Korea. There she completed her master's degree in divinity and continued with the mission work she had previously been involved in with my dad. It was in the process of this service, almost eight years to the date after my father's untimely demise, in December 2004, that she was also involved in a strange and fatal car accident and died. I, again not by my choice, became the unlikely head of our surviving family. Many dark years followed. I cannot articulate them except by sharing the lyrics of the title song of the first album I was able to record in the US over a decade after all these events.

Through the love of Christ our Savior,
All will be well,
Free and changeless is His favor;
All, all is well.
Precious is the blood that healed us, perfect is the grace that sealed us,
Strong the hand stretched forth to shield us,
All must be well.

Though we pass through tribulation.
All will be well,
Ours is such a full salvation;
All, all is well.

Happy, still in God confiding,
Fruitful, if in Christ abiding,
Holy, through the Spirit's guiding,
All must be well.

We expect a bright tomorrow;
All will be well,
Faith can sing through days of sorrow,
All, all is well.
On our Father's love relying,
Jesus every need supplying, or in living, or in dying,
All must be well.
(Mary Bowley Peters, 1847)

It would take my siblings and me many more years to recover from all these happenings and the accompanying distress. God again brought us through. We all fully pushed forward, pressing on into our God-given destinies. After so many years of losses, brokenness, and other family tragedies, we finally overcame as a family. People can be killed, but God's word cannot be killed. We are all continuing to fulfill God's purpose and destiny, daily manifesting His glory. The enemy attacked and made major assaults against our faith in Christ and our family structure. It was an attempt to stop Christ's call on our lives, but God brought us through, kept us together, and led us in His triumphant victory.

All manner of violent deaths and inexplicable sufferings were also experienced by the early apostles of our Lord Jesus Christ. The spiritual principle that I very gently and humbly offer to any Christian facing the heavy weight of persecution or the painful agony of grief is found in John 1:5. In the darkness, God is still our light.

The light shines in the darkness, and the darkness has not overcome it. (John 1:5, NIV)

Even when I walk through the darkest valley, I will not be afraid, for you are close beside me. Your rod and your staff protect and comfort me. (Psalm 23:4, NLT)

Blessed are those who mourn, for they will be comforted. (Matthew 5:4, NIV)

Faith in Christ, humor, optimism, strength, an outstanding work ethic, and all of the real estate they had personally acquired were all part of the legacy our precious parents left us. Today all four of their children still continue to serve the Lord.

Chapter Seventeen

GOD'S EARLY PREPARATION

Before I conclude by offering you a glimpse into our faith diary, I want to go back in time,"

To prepare us before we permanently left England in 1995, not yet fully knowing that we were about to embark on a great adventure of faith, God brought us many new books. They came across our path in various ways, such as through friends and acquaintances, and unbeknownst to us prepared us for our new life. We suddenly encountered through these books the awesome testimonies of some of God's faithful servants. They were real-life faith encounters and accounts of their lives, much like those in the Bible, but for our times—men and women who had wholly surrendered their lives in complete obedience to God's word. One of the books we were blessed to read was the faith account of George Muller, a Christian evangelist and director of the Ashley Down orphanage in Bristol, England. We read how, through prayer and faith, he had built orphanages housing tens of thousands of children in England in the nineteenth century. Another book was titled *Exodus II*, an account of the faith walk of Steve Lightle.

God sent us His word in so many ways and performed many wonderful acts to propel us forward into this new supernatural way of life previously unknown to us. What does living by faith day-to-day really look like in past and modern times? Having read some of the diaries of faith that these believers had left behind for us, and being so greatly encouraged and strengthened by their journeys, we decided to keep a diary for some years of some of our day-to-day experiences.

We knew that our recollection of many events might fade with time. We did not want to forget how desperately we needed and relied on God so many times, and we wanted to instantly capture the sentiments of those moments. He faithfully always came through and will come through for you.

Recorded here are some of our day-to-day activities, written in quick scribbles in various notebooks. We share some of these intimate details of our lives with you in order that you can follow the idea of God's early preparation, which encourages those who have received "word" from God regarding their purposes and callings. If you desire to walk in complete obedience to Him, be confident that the God who calls you is faithful, and trust the God of the impossible in every area of your life. Obtain victory over doubt, fear, and any other spiritual warfare with unswerving, unwavering, childlike faith in the everlasting word of God. Trust in the unchanging faithfulness of God's character. The God of Abraham, our father in the faith, is still the same God we believe in and serve today. Praise the Lord!

> It was by faith that Abraham obeyed when God called him to leave home and go to another land that God would give him as his inheritance. He went without knowing where he was going. (Hebrews 11:8, NLT)

> Jesus Christ is the same yesterday and today and forever. (Hebrews 13:8, NIV)

> Faith is the confidence that what we hope for will actually happen; it gives us assurance about things we cannot see. (Hebrews 11:1, NLT)

My husband Jide recorded the first part of our faith diary while in London. He had to temporarily return there in 1999 to renew our paperwork after our first sponsors reneged on their promise. Left with a huge immigration nightmare that lasted over a decade, we pressed forward into God's promise.

Chapter Eighteen

FAITH DIARY

Feburary 1, 1999, London, UK—Jide writes, "For the last three weeks all I can say is that the Lord has been good. I have experienced His love, provision, and guidance. He has been causing things to fall into place. I have been able to communicate with my wife and children in California and am constantly reminding myself of my visions from Him and the many dreams He has shown me. I felt physically down yesterday and this morning, but after reading the word, I know what He has promised will come to pass in our lives. My job is to diligently listen to Him, give the Lord undivided attention, and obey. Remembering that He, the Lord, is faithful, I must listen to and obey his voice.

I still began to question and doubt some of God's promises to us.

February 2—The Lord has provided for me for the few months that I will be in England. I obtained a temporary place to work while waiting for our visas to be processed. It was a place that was my very heart's desire in accordance with His prophetic Word. Praise Jesus! I have surrendered all.

February 3—Thanks be to God! Bukky and children are fine. His wisdom has kept my wife and children.

February 29—I finally received our visa from the embassy here in London! The Lord gave us more than I asked!

March 1—Trusting Jesus and praising Him concerning my wife and children. I *know* He loves each one of us (2 Chronicles 20).

March 2—The Lord is God! I received a call from Bukky—all is well. The night before, we were totally unsure how things would work out. My trust is *totally in Jesus.* "Give us aid against the enemy, for human help is worthless" (Psalm 60:11, NIV). My wife tells me that accommodation for the month is settled, and we have a car to use for another week! I bless the Lord.

March 7—Left England gloriously. Arrived safely back home to California! Thanking you so much, Lord. My wife picked me up from Los Angeles airport.

Diary now continues with me (Bukky) in California from March 9, 1999—Praise Jesus, *we bought a car!* All glory and praise to Jesus. Trusting Him to complete the work He began in and through us. "Being confident of this, that he who began a good work in you will carry it on to completion until the day of Christ Jesus" (Philippians 1:6, NIV).

March 10—Praise God. Got a call from the car company with a better deal on the car! Just resting in and praising Jesus.

March 17—Praise Jesus! The Lord provided $1,200. In the midst of a phone call to a pastor regarding a donation they were sending to us, they had at first thought it was $200, checked again, and it was actually $1,200, to the amazement of the speaker! Our car transaction completed and settled today.

March 22—With our paperwork now updated, we are trusting the Lord for Jide to obtain a new permanent employment position and funds to celebrate our daughter's birthday. The fuel in the new car is on quarter. We have risen on this new day with great hope and expectation.

March 22 (10:00 p.m.)—Praise the Lord! He has worked a miracle in our accounts. Money in hand and a full tank of gas. Praising Jesus. Thank the Lord for victory

March 23—We have $100 left over in hand. The Holy Spirit directed us, "Don't eat your seed." So we gave $50 to a Christian ministry. We are awaiting funds to cover all our bills, renew my [Bukky'] expired passport, extend our car insurance, and are still believing for Jide's new employment in our new land. Just watching God move.

March 23 (5:00 p.m.)—Praising God! Received $100 in love gifts and $25 money order from someone in Seattle. Sowed $45 (tithe and offering); trusting the Lord for increase.

March 27—Praise Jesus! Jide received an offer of employment. Just as God had spoken to us over three years ago in Costa Mesa. My passport renewal application has also been sent. Jide received $100 in love gifts from speaking at a men's breakfast.

March 28—We have decided, according to the direction of the Holy Spirit, to send $70 to a church in Mission Viejo's building fund. We are trusting in Jesus for all our outstanding bills to be paid and starting a three-day fast beginning on Monday. Praise the Lord!

March 29—Funds on hold, we are unable to withdraw the $100 received. We had about $3 to manage for the day. (The Lord blessed it—even obtained a free pack of hot dogs from the store due to their mistake in price marking.) Just received a phone call promising over $300 in love gift donations. We are trusting God for His wisdom and understanding.

March 30—Praise the Lord. Sowed our seed. The Lord provided for the day. Our hope is built on nothing less than Jesus' blood and righteousness.

March 31—Trusting Jesus to supply all needs. Got a new insurance deal lined up (saved $600), always believing God to supply all our needs according to His riches in glory.

April 1—Praise Jesus! A sister in the Lord was directed to bless us with groceries and $85 in vouchers. Praising Jesus for all His faithfulness! Found out this month that the door that had opened for Jide's employment had closed. We just wait on Jesus, while continuing to minister, nothing unusual.

April 3—Went grocery shopping. Praise God. Trusting Jesus to supply all needs.

April 5—Jide received a call for a job—but it was again canceled before concluding. Still praising Jesus, we received someone's seed today for $40 and sowed $30 into a Christian ministry. Trusting Jesus to meet all our needs. Believing for an additional $3,000 today; again our hope is built on nothing less than Jesus' blood and righteousness.

April 6—Praise God! The Lord opened a new door for Jide to work in another temporary position for about three months. Starting today.

April 8—Our message beeper was disconnected. Then we received the check in the mail from the church in Pomona for $120, cashed it, and paid up the beeper.

April 9—*Praise God!* Jide collected his very first paycheck from working in the USA. We sowed it *all* to *Jesus in faith*. Heard from the church in Pomona that had blessed us in the past that they are commencing support for us again, and they had just mailed us $120. Praising God! Jide received a call for a pre interview. Resting in Jesus.

April 10—Sowed $300 to Christian ministry. Declared a day's fast unto the Lord. Awaiting God's miracles, always trusting and believing in Him to meet every need.

April 11—Just waiting on Jesus for all needs. We know He is faithful. Praising God! Trusting Him to meet all payments!

April 16—Found out a few days ago that it takes at least two months for the issuing of the renewed passport that I needed to complete, but Jesus has raised up help and we are trusting Him for a miracle. Staying in. Trusting Him . . . to the limit. Resting in Him . . . believing for God's favor in banks/systems, etc.!

April 17—I was told this week that my passport would be issued, and I would receive it on Monday or Tuesday! The Lord opened a door of ministry at the church in Pomona. We are again trusting God for His miracles as we put in an application for a new place. Trusting God for all the necessary payments.

April 18—Praise the Lord! Had a "Holy Ghost" time at the Pomona Church. Got a call during the week from the apartment company saying, "Very good credit report, all is in order," just to fax the letter we have. Trusting God for all the necessary paperwork to be physically sealed by Monday. Who is wonderful? It's Jesus! Praying to the Lord for further direction.

April 19—Received a call from a church (we were trusting the Lord for $1,550), and they told us they have $900 in donations and gifts for us. By evening time, operating in the Lord's given wisdom, we had a promise to receive $1,650 more from other sources by April 30. Praise God! We spent the night in the Lake Forest area. Got the last nonsmoking room at a very nice hotel through the Lord's favor. God kindly enabled us to rest.

April 24—Praise God! I received my updated I-94 [an immigration document]. More than we asked for! Just returned from Mexico.

April 27—Today we had planned to fast and pray, but we allowed the enemy to hinder us with division. We are trusting in the mercies of God. Jesus has given us victory—by faith.

April 27 (evening)—Battle over and won, forever. Praise God!

April 28—Jide now also known at his new place of work as minister of the Gospel, was told today by boss of another company, "We *must* talk."

April 30—Moved into our new place. Beautiful! Trusting the Lord for furniture. We know it's a new day and are thankful to Jesus. I received my new passport! It was processed in less than three weeks, compared to the normal two months. Got our new phone line installed. Jide was also asked to submit his resume to a new employer. Trusting God for a permanent, higher-paying position for him, we know He is faithful. Got our furniture! Received a call from one of our partners in Texas. I had planned to send out letters yesterday after another partner had called us, confirming God's will for our mail-out. The Lord is simply blessing what we have and multiplying it. We are sure of His

mercies and provision. The Lord told us to say
"We have more than enough," for our God is a
more-than-enough God.

May 1–13—(Housing) Our biggest bill was
paid without a thought at the beginning of the
month. I have sent in my renewed passport to
request our required additional visas. Not happy
to find out a vital piece of information our
agent did not tell us. We have just discovered
that, due to our ignorance of the area, our new
address puts us in the wrong school district for
our son's school. Our ignorance had given the
enemy room to try and remove our son from
his awesome school. Thank the Lord for giving
us His forgiveness and favor! We fought and
gained the victory for him to stay at his school,
avoiding the huge disruption to his education.
We have requested to come out of the contract without penalties, but the management
declined. But we know who the Lord is and are
trusting Jesus about our next move. Praying for
His direction and provision. Our car stopped
working on May 10. The Lord opened our eyes
to how and where we should get it towed for
fixing. It was repaired the next day with a bill
of $0.00. Praise Jesus! Trusting Him for Jide's
well-paying, permanent employment position.

May 14—I met with the director of one of our city's largest charitable organizations for homeless families and discovered that God has given me favor and a voice in our city! Our eyes are on Him. The Lord spoke to Jide in a dream that he should stand up now, because now is his future.

May 19—Jide had an interview and received new employment! Waiting to find out the start date! Praise God!

May 21—As of today, we have submitted our notice to quit our "wrong district" residence to ensure our son can continue at his school. Today we signed the paperwork for a new house. Trusting and praying for God's provision.

May 28—We have exercised our faith and fasted over the first house we found and believe it's not God's will *at this time*, so we have shifted our focus. I discovered and found a much better deal than we had ever heard of. We have put down our deposit in faith and are trusting him for the completion (besides paycheck). We know our God is a miracle-working God.

June 4—The Lord has been moving wonderfully! Prophetic words/dreams received earlier in the year are beginning to take shape and manifest. We are just flowing with His Spirit and trusting that He who began the good work will finish it and not one of His promises fail!

June 7—As of today, the funds for the deposit check for our new place are in the bank! Received a call yesterday that has released to us, by His grace, a continuous financial blessing—Praise the Lord!

The Lord gave us strategies for ministry:

Train church "members" to have the mindset that they are to be ministers, meeting the needs of people in their various spheres of influence under their church leadership's spiritual covering. Jide and I are working together, and taking responsibility for prayer and evangelism. Everything has a beginning point. Before a person can become a professor, kindergarten, elementary, or primary school is a must. First things must be completed first; they are the route to greater things—every little step we all take toward our call is significant.

"Do not despise these small beginnings, for the LORD rejoices to see the work

begin, to see the plumb line in Zerub-
babel's hand. (The seven lamps repre-
sent the eyes of the LORD that search
all around the world" (Zechariah 4:10,
NLT).

The local church is the base for global ministry.
Plan to open a prayer line
Pray for evangelistic strategies for our city and
beyond.

June 11—Tithes due as of today from love gifts
we received are $111. The Lord has given us
wisdom pertaining to our move. Praise Jesus
again for His continued supply of wisdom and
riches to fulfill his call. This week the Lord
released funds to us from ministry and from
work. We praise Jesus always for His supply
and guidance.

June 16—Paid the love gift tithes due ($111).
Trusting Jesus for $1,150 for some furnishings
for our newest place on or before June 18. I
received a very special blessing with regard to
extending my driver's license, while still completing all necessary immigration paperwork—
God has planted us. We receive it by faith, now
we expect *manifestation*!

June 17—Jide was moved by the Holy Spirit to go to a prayer/Bible study. The word was about Joseph and all that he went through to obtain and fulfill God's promise.

> He sent a man before them, Joseph, who was sold as a slave. They afflicted his feet with fetters, He himself was laid in irons; until the time that his word came to pass, The word of the LORD tested him The king sent and released him, The ruler of peoples, and set him free. He made him lord of his house and ruler over all his possession. (Psalm 105:17–21, NASB)

Jide was also blessed to receive $100 for the ministry. Praise Jesus.

June 18 (8:30 a.m.)—Our phone line has now been transferred to our new place. We have $350 less than we need after all the penalties and so forth . . . We are trusting Jesus that in *this* day, we will have more than enough. Signed all the new papers and finally began our move today. *All* of our help comes from God and we are trusting Him.

June 18 (11:15 a.m.)—*Praise God!* We have all the funds needed. The Lord gave me wisdom and favor, and amidst our praise we received our miracle!

June 18 (5:45 p.m.)—Received the keys (two sets) and moved in!

June 20—We have completed the move! Praise God! (Today was the last day of the *special* deal!) Submitted keys back to the old place. Went to view properties for our new ministry meetings!—Praise God!

June 21—I continue to travel and minister, and Jide started his new job, much more than we both expected. Thank you, Jesus!

June 26—We put in an offer for our new ministry meeting space. The Lord opened the door to make known our need for new office furniture, and we are trusting Him to meet every need.

June 24—Had $10 left after meeting all our personal and ministry commitments—we are trusting Jesus for all our needs to be met by the end of the day. As a result of hearing the voice

of the Spirit, we received $450 today. God is
wonderful.

July 2—Praise God! We have been experiencing the goodness of the Lord. The brakes on the
car wore out, and the windshield steamed up.
We took it to the dealer and dealt with some
confusion, but the Lord repaired our car with
another bill of $0.00! Spent $26 on oil change
and had the use of a Park Avenue for two days!!
The Lord is enlarging our coast and mindset!
We received a donation of some beautiful office
furniture, and the Lord even sent someone to
help us unload the truck! The truck itself was
given for the move at no charge—God's favor!
As of today, all our bills have been paid! We
know El Shaddai is our source and have been
reminded of the Lord's promise. If we hearken
to His voice and obey His commands, we will
lend to many nations and borrow from none!

> If only you fully obey the LORD your
> God and are careful to follow all these
> commands I am giving you today. For
> the LORD your God will bless you
> as he has promised, and you will lend
> to many nations but will borrow from
> none. You will rule over many nations

but none will rule over you. (Deuteronomy 15:5–6, NIV)

July 10—Praise Him again! Today we received
the agreement from the landlord for leasing a
property for ministry use! The Lord miracu-
lously supplied the paperwork and a partner to
sign the lease with. We are thanking God for
His favor and now await for the funds ($5,000)
to be transferred from our Father's heavenly
account (His riches in glory) to our earthly
bank account. We know it's the Lord's building! "And my God will meet all your needs
according to the riches of his glory in Christ
Jesus" (Philippians 4:19, NIV).

July 13—Praising Jesus! After all expenses paid,
we have gone from $5 and half a tank of gas to
$500. Praise God for His provision!

July 15—As of today, all papers regarding lease
on our part have been signed. The Lord has
opened our eyes as to which insurance company
to use. Once again we are seeing that everything
we did in the past, which at the time seemed
fruitless, is now fruitful and is a blessing to us.
The steps of a righteous man are ordered by the
Lord. "The LORD directs the steps of the godly.

He delights in every detail of their lives" (Psalm 37:23, NLT). Our lesson—no need to pray for a miracle for things that you can receive from the Lord by doing things properly and waiting for the right timing.

July 30—Praise the Lord! Jide had been saying just yesterday that the income from his new company and our ministry was not yet enough to cover all expenses, but God reminded him that *He* is our source, and He will provide any way He chooses. We were able to replace the battery in the car. The Lord had provided for it way ahead of time. Children have both started at a new school. Thank you, Lord! And we must remember, that it has not been by might or power but by His Spirit. Once again we thank God for all my ministry invitations and Jide's employment. Everything is proving to be a miracle of God's love and favor.

Trusting for increase on every side!

We received $250 in the mail, and a check for $1,160. We give glory, honor, and thanks always to Jesus our Lord for His care.

August 2—Received $200 more in the mail! I just keep thanking Him for our ever-increasing harvest.

August 3—The Spirit of the Lord woke us up to pray together at 3:00 a.m. It has been quite a while since that has happened. We know that all the praying we have done has been by His grace! Received health insurance for family. We thank Jehovah Rapha who has kept us in divine health all these years.

August 5—Praise the Lord! Some funds we were expecting to come in have not yet come, but we praise God for the lesson we learned through the experience. Now more than ever simply on guard, watching, lest we fall back. On a lighter note, we obtained a portrait deal from the Internet. Thank God for persistence—discovered it and ended the day booking the appointment for all of us! We took professional family pictures; the steps of the righteous are ordered by the Lord.

August 16—There was a temporary delay in receiving Jide's wages. Praising God for another lesson learned about a bird in hand, but we know Jesus is our source. Made a late payment on a bill that was due. Just praising Jesus that my brother Muyiwa arrived in California safely to visit with us; we thank you Lord!

September 1–8—Jide had some trouble at his workplace that the Lord had previously given us a heads-up about. Through God's grace, what the enemy meant for evil, the Lord has turned it around for good! Hallelujah!

September 17—Again we praise the Lord anyway. We found out that our healthcare plan was not correctly in place. I was not feeling well but was unable to receive care through our insurance coverage. We pressed in all day and finally received more—I was able to see a doctor who turned out to be a Christian. We now have a new medical group just around the corner from us! Thanking God for healing through every means He provides.

September 21—A man ran into the back of our car today. Great impact, but little damage to our car and no one was injured. Praise God. I got out and immediately prayed with the man who had run into us. I also got a report from my doctor, suspecting some health concern. We prayed under the unction of the Holy Spirit that no evil report would be found. The next day I received the all clear! Praise God!

September 29—Received $500 from the insurance company as compensation toward any additional medical treatment for the accident after they had fixed the car. I was also blessed with $200 from one of my ministry engagements and a $50 love gift as a result of meeting with a lady for her counseling.

September 30—Trying times at work for Jide. He's now increased his vigilance and diligence. We are trusting the Lord for his promotion.

October 2—Trusting God for the continuing rejuvenation of our marital relationship and for financial increase to meet certain needs and balance personal and ministry budgets. We have agreed to separate tithes from offerings as we continue to give. We wait on Him.

October 9—Thanking God! We received two checks in the mail, totaling $2,000.

October 10—Three-day prayer and fasting. Have collected the repaired car after the accident in perfect condition.

The Lord had also made provision for us to have the use of another car from September

28–October 18. Thank God for all His provision, favor, and wisdom.

Oct 23—With a few days left to make some payments before the due dates, we trusted the Lord, and He came through again!

November—Jide experiencing the grace of God at work, and the Lord worked all the recent hardships together for his good. "And we know that God causes everything to work together for the good of those who love God and are called according to his purpose for them" (Romans 8:28, NLT).

December 13—We trusted that the Lord would provide through Jide's work and all other avenues especially before Christmas, and Jide received his biggest pay increase ever! Praising Jesus.

Dec 14—The Lord says, "He has blessed my husband's work and has made him the head and not the tail"—expecting it to manifest!!

> The LORD will make you the head, not the tail. If you pay attention to the commands of the LORD your God

that I give you this day and carefully follow them, you will always be at the top, never at the bottom. (Deuteronomy 28:13, NIV)

Dec 22—Praise God! I spoke to my mother in Korea! Trusting the Lord for her ministry there. The Lord has done marvelous things. We are grateful and glad! The Lord again shows me that persecutions of Christians in Nigeria will greatly increase. We have decided to pray for the nations every Friday. The old year is done and the year 2000 begins. Thank you, Lord, for again seeing us through!

January 15, 2000—Within three days of a pastor friend's mentioning that she would like Jide and me to do a teaching on a particular subject, Jide heard a well-respected radio preacher teaching the same subject! Then I was suddenly blessed to receive an unsolicited book on the same subject. We praise God who confirms and ordains our way.

February 13—Visited and ministered at a new church. Had a wonderful time in the Lord. Received a love gift of $300.

February 14—Jide and I went out for a meal together on St. Valentine's Day.

February 16—Jide received his paycheck. All worked out well! Always Praising Jesus.

February 17—Jide was called into boss's office and commended for work done and given a $2,500 raise to his salary. We thank the Lord for promotion and increase.

February 24—As of today, our mother in Korea is doing well. The Lord is working in her life.

I am due to restart my voice lessons on the 26th. All our bills are paid, and the Lord has given favor as regarding filing our tax returns (in progress).

Children are doing well in school and a bully in our son's new class is now (in his words) a good boy!

Jide was commended at work by another boss in response to an email. We thank God for His grace. The Lord just opened more new doors. Our focus is ever on Him.

March 2—I'm getting ready to host our very first Women of Destiny Conference 2000. Preparations have commenced with speed and favor. Tremendous responses from many ladies.

March 4—Praise Jesus, on March 2, Jide was given another raise! $10,000 increase—with a promotion! The Lord helped and made his first major responsibility a success. His offices have now been moved to the 8th floor. New beginnings and trusting Jesus for increase in His wisdom, anointing, and favor.

March 5—We received $150 from a sister in the Lord, a gift springing from ministry she had received from me. A prophetic word was also released pertaining to my connecting with a large, well-known ministry. My ministry assignment now has a global reach! Praise Jesus.

March 8—We collected the first contributions toward the Women of Destiny Conference, gathering $440.

March 10—Received a letter from the DMV stating that our stay in US had been verified. Trusting Jesus to receive permanent California driver's license.

March 11—During the week, Pastor Bakare was visiting Los Angeles and, by the grace of God, I got to see him briefly. He is such a blessing in our lives and to the body of Christ. The meeting was indeed a divine connection, providing covering for another believer in the Lord who was going to Nigeria and was in need of his always kind assistance.

March 16—Glory to God! Jide's promotion at work was made public. The Lord said to him not to be afraid—He is the one promoting him by making his employers recognize the work he had been doing.

March 20—The Lord gave wisdom that released $833 to us. The money required for the part of the deposits needed for the conference, that is due by April 1, but God has already provided!

I have begun to get stirrings toward more ministry to Kenyans. While writing a letter to a minister in Kenya one afternoon, another Kenyan minister called the same day, saying she had dreamed about me that afternoon.

March 21—Jide received information regarding some Kenyans!

March 22—I "happened" to meet a bishop from Kenya.

March 24—The Lord opened a door. We went to preach in San Bernardino, California. Saw souls saved and baptized with the Holy Spirit. Had a wonderful time with them. I was reminded that having authority in Christ does *not* mean we are effectively using it.

March Ends—Praise Jesus! Celebrated a decade of being together this year.

April 2—Praise God—Received a call from South Korea. A woman desired a baby. We received prophetic strategy to fast for one day and watch God move! We are blessing Jesus in advance for the victory!

April 5—I had decided in my heart to give a gift of $100 to a pastor on Friday. By the evening, Jide came home with $100 surprise cash gift he had received! Lord Jesus, thank you.

April 10—Our son woke up from sleep with a memory verse: 2 Chronicles 20:20—"Believe in The LORD God and be established."

April 14—The number of women from the gathering has now increased! We are believing for a full house! Yesterday I prayed in my heart regarding our getting a music system, at that very same time Jide had received one as a gift. Wow!

Sudden spiritual warfare! Our daughter broke her wrist while playing at home. It's a day we are fasting. We are not moved. Her spirits were also not dampened. We took her to the hospital. Her arm was placed in a splint. Told to go to our doctor on Monday to confirm.

April 17—Doctor x-rayed the wrist and showed it to us, confirming that the bone was indeed broken. He referred us to an orthopedic hospital and specialist for final analysis and to put it in a cast.

April 19—*We prayed and praised Jesus!* We took our daughter to the orthopedic specialist, but he could not detect a broken bone in his new x-ray. Our daughter was in no pain and instead of putting her arm into a cast, the splint was removed; she is fine! Throughout the ordeal she was continually praying and thanking the Lord for healing her arm, and it manifested! Again, "Wow, Lord! The previously taken x-rays clearly showed a broken bone, but the one on this visit showed none! Hallelujah! Jehovah Rapha still heals today! The Lord heals us.

Who forgives all your sins and heals all
your diseases. (Psalm 103:3, NIV)

And the prayer offered in faith will
make the sick person well; the Lord will
raise them up. If they have sinned, they
will be forgiven. (James 5:15, NIV)

April 21—We have both finally received our
California permanent driver's licenses! Praise
God.

May 4—We now have the total number of
women for our Women of Destiny Conference.
My brother Muyiwa will fly in from England
to lead the services in music for the praise and
worship.

May 12—Jide and I have agreed to sow a very
substantial seed into a ministry that helps the
homeless and hungry. We are believing in the
Lord for the miraculous provision of this seed.
We prayed and took communion, inviting the
Lord's presence into our agreement before Him.

May 15—Praising Jesus! All arrangements for
the women's conference are going smoothly,
and there has been no stress. Sadly, I received

sudden news of the untimely passing away of my young uncle in Nigeria.

May 25—I dreamed last night of the maintenance man for our house fixing something. "He had dug up some concrete in the dream. It was right after Jide and I had spoken privately in the early hours of the morning about our needing an additional phone line.

Real Time! Our maintenance man came and fixed our phone lines, giving us telephone extensions in the living and bedrooms at no charge! This is the 5th day of our seven-day fast, and it has been the easiest. Thank you, Lord.

June 1—Jide and I received our prayed-for seed from the Lord and presented our promised substantial gift seed to the ministry the Lord led us to. We thank Jesus for His provision of the seed. The Lord has also given favor with regard to the renewing of Jide's passport. It has been sent off. The Lord has given us new fervor to "lend to many and borrow from none." Be debt free.

June 2—Praising Jesus! All necessary bills are paid! We have decided to wait on Jesus with regard to a house. Our eyes are on Him.

June 8—I received an invitation to attend and speak at a major charity event being held at the largest Marriott Hotel in our city. We are still receiving inquiries from people who want to attend the women's conference. Jesus is awesome! Received the use of a PA system from a brother.

June 11—Praise God! The Women of Destiny conference was a great success! Many ladies shared with us of their encounters with God, awesome! We were able to completely sponsor three of the ladies with all their expenses paid. My brother Muyiwa came from London! We were blessed to collect and bless him with a love offering. Donations received far exceeded anything we have ever been blessed with or could have hoped for—no one like Jesus! A $5,000 personal gift was also given to me by an attendee who said the Lord prompted her to do so in obedience to Him.

During this conference I also prophesied over my brother Muyiwa. Releasing God's words of guidance to him on the three areas he would need to do things differently from what he had set his heart upon, for the future enlargement of his ministry and career. God has something big for his future! The Lord confirmed these words to him through a phone call he received from his friend here in the USA before he left. He has returned safely to the UK.

2015 Update: As I now write this memoir in 2015, all the prophecies I spoke over my brother Muyiwa's life at that special event have come to pass. He is now a television host on one of the Christian Broadcasting Network's (An American Christian Television Network) flagship programs in Africa and the UK. He always testifies about the "prophetess" at a women's conference in California who told him his future. It was at this special event. We Praise God that all His promises are true!

2021 Update: My brother Muyiwa was awarded an OBE by Elizabeth II in her 2020 birthday honors list. Wow! All of the glory and honor go to God.

June 26—2nd day of praise and deliverance fast (Esther). We have had communion with the Lord and have set our hearts on sowing a large seed to the Los Angeles Missions. Trusting God for it to be established. We are expecting miracles! Praising Jesus always! (Hallelujah)

June 29—Reminded ourselves of a previous decision we made and decided that God's will is for us to be in position in the following areas.

Complete all immigration processes

Be debt free

Move from the apartment and settle our children in a house. Praise God for His wisdom; we received a $300 gift voucher. Thank you, Lord!

July 3—The Lord spoke to us to start to hold evangelistic gatherings and begin by working with the churches we have a relationship with. He has spoken that we would go to many different nations, preaching salvation.

July 5—Praise God! All debts are paid and canceled! We had a credit check run for a new three-bedroom place and report was great. Praise the Lord!

July 6—Found a two-bedroom townhouse instead in an area the Lord had previously spoken to us of. We are going to do the paperwork tomorrow. Praising and trusting Jesus!

July 7—Signed all the paperwork and waiting for the contracts to be completed.

July 8—Our offer has been accepted! We have a new house exactly in the area where the Lord spoke to us of. Glory to God in the highest!

July 15—Moved out of the apartment and into our God-given townhouse. We call it Isaac 1.

July 19—Praise God! Jide got blessed by his boss. He was told that his domain at work would be increased.

August 1—We are hearing of and seeing more manifestations of prophetic words spoken over the lives of women who attended the women's conference. One of the ladies is finally relocating to Oklahoma, just like God had said she would.

With regards to the evangelistic gatherings (harvest campaigns), we have spoken to the first pastor the Lord laid on our hearts and his words have confirmed our thoughts. We are looking toward the beginning in the month of September.

September 25—Divinely received the name of the guest speaker of the next Woman of Destiny Conference for 2001! According to God's leading, we had found out her contact address and sent a letter of invitation to her. Praise God! Invitation accepted! We have also seen tremendous improvement in our son's academic abilities. We are seeing the word of God manifest in our lives daily! The Lord has given us the strategy to obtain the gifts we want to bless the ladies with for the Women of Destiny Conference 2001.

October 5—Praise God! We have received the children's documentation for our tax paperwork by acting on information received.

October 13—We have sent off Ebun and Remi's passports for renewal. (No charge was necessary.)

October 23—Jide saw "Judas" spirit exposed at work, and the Lord gave him victory! The Lord had revealed this to us a few days prior. Thank you, Lord!

November 16—We received back Ebun and Remi's renewed passports. After the victory at work, Jide just received a salary increase of $5000, with a $1,000 bonus. Great is the Lord.

December 18, 2000—Jide received an award from his company's circle of honor as the employee of the year for his excellent work. We give all the glory to Jesus. We have sent off all necessary tax forms. Now awaiting tax returns.

Happy New Year! 2001 is finally here!

February 3, 2001—Still praising God! Through the Lord's guidance, we found a printer to print the Women of Destiny gathering flyers. Two thousand have been printed, and as of today 1,800 have been distributed, locally and overseas. We are now just resting in Jesus and believing in Him for great things. The printer even asked us not to be concerned with the bill until we begin receiving registrations. Praise the Lord!

February 8—Received a letter from the immigration services stating that our petition had again been denied on the grounds that we had filed using the wrong forms! The previous night we had spent time in worship. We know whom we have believed. I have received a prophetic leading from the Lord that Jide was to ask for a meeting with his boss and request the company's sponsorship instead of our going through the churches. His appointment is set for tomorrow at 10:30 a.m. to request his bosses' assistance on the denial.

February 9—*Praise Jesus*! Before my husband had even finished asking to place a request to the company for the sponsoring of our family's permanent immigration status the boss said yes! We are determined to see God's promise fulfilled. All systems are again go!

February 16—Praise God! Jide was called in by his boss and told good and bad news. Good: They will sponsor us for our green cards. Bad: They could no longer allow him to continue working until all the necessary paperwork was completed. More tough times before getting to the other side.

February 17—Praise Jesus. Sent off first of the needed documents to get us back into the system.

February 18—I had planned to go to Florida but, because of the change in our financial circumstances, I am now unsure whether I should go or not. We are trusting Jesus for direction and a way to be made. We had also planned for this week to be a seven-day fast to seek the Lord. We are excited to see Him move!

February 20—Praise God. We began the first day of our fast. I am in Florida. Had a wonderful trip and discovered the Lord had healed me from extreme fatigue and pain in my ears during flights. Jesus is awesome. Trusting Jesus. We listened once again to God's prophetic words given to us years back that we had recorded on audio cassette tapes to remind ourselves that His plan has not changed.

February 21—I met a lady in Florida who picked me up and dropped me off for all the meetings. I hate driving in new places, and our Heavenly Father took care of that, too. God bless the lady from Arkansas. We know that we are in the Lord's will and are continuously seeking His face, and trusting and following Him. His purpose for us is perfect!

February 24—Praise God! I also met another lady who expressed an interest in coming to the next Women of Destiny conference and would be bringing four friends from the Bahamas with her. I had a desire for chicken and rice, but not knowing the area, I didn't know where to go. God is so kind, He led the same lady to meet my humble need. He always takes care of His children!

February 27—Thank you, Lord! I am back in California from the visit to Florida! All praise to God. I had an excellent journey.

March 7—I dreamed of one of our disciples, who also said she had dreamed about me just a few days ago! I have set up Saturday for a Bible study in their home. This is the 1st day of our three-day fast asking God for more ministry doors to open, and the final completion and manifestation of all our immigration needs. Also God's wisdom for all those working on it.

March 18—The Lord's favor has been upon me, and He has most wonderfully strengthened us. Trusting the Lord for more doors. Our ministry diary has been increasing. Hallelujah!

March 24—Just remembered our receiving a $100 cash love gift in the mail from Korea! God is awesome and can come from *anywhere*!

March 27—Praise Jesus! Received $250. We thank the Lord for His favor. Had fellowship at a ministry partner's house. Jesus is wonderful.

March 30—Received $151 more in the mail.

April 1—We will begin our forty-day fast. Seeking Jesus for His grace. We desire more of Him.

April 10—Sent out partner's letters for sponsorship of the next Women of Destiny Conference under the Lord's anointing.

April 14—As of today, Jide received two new job opportunities—the Lord's leading is that these are not for us. Trusting Jesus for provision and direction. We have entered our 14th day of fasting, knowing His presence and grace.

April 17—Trusting Jesus for a mighty manifestation of His Spirit at the women's conference and everywhere we go in awesome ways. We are giving our all to Him.

April 23—Jide was shown in a dream that our green card applications were approved by the *power of God!*

April 28—We received $1,460 in the mail from our ministry assignments. Was expecting $1,000 but received more. Thank you, Lord.

April 29—Praise Jesus for a fulfilled ministry engagement. God's presence was awesome! I spoke on Worship. Was blessed to receive $300 as a gift, and new ministry partners signed up with their monthly support and pledges.

May 6—Praise God! Had a wonderful time in the Lord at the San Bernardino church. Gave $200 to their building fund and gave them back their love gift to us of $150. We also sowed some suits that God had laid on Jide's heart to give. They were his best ones. Rejoicing in Him—hallelujah.

Received word from mum in Korea that she had started work in the seminary over there. Praise the Lord.

May 11—Returned to San Bernardino for a preaching engagement. The Lord released $500 to us from my ministry at a woman's Bible study. Thank you, Lord!

May 22—Praise our Heavenly Father. We have obtained an additional six women (one from Ohio) attending the Women of Destiny Conference. Also received a $200 love gift from a "mother in Israel" last Sunday. We praise the Lord for gathering His women.

June 3—Praise the Lord. Great excitement is in the air with regard to our upcoming women's conference—payments coming in. Our tickets are being purchased. Everyone has a spirit of expectancy.

June 17—Just finished a three-day fast. The enemy tried to aggravate us in the midst of it—but we are no longer ignorant of the wiles of the devil. Experienced some last-minute cancellations/rearrangements in the women conference's which has led to a $300 blessing in the form of savings. "And we know that in all things God works for the good of those who love him, who have been called according to his purpose" (Romans 8:28, NIV).

The Lord is providing for all of our needs, and we are walking in His Spirit of wisdom. Received word from Korea that our mother has now been made a pastor in the seminary.

Everyone appears to be doing well in Christ. Praise God.

June 20—The Lord has given us Genesis 22:14, "The LORD will provide," as our family's memory verse today regarding the women's conference. Wow! I went out after hearing the verse and found a $1 bill caught between two hedges by the post office! We know the Lord has provided us a ram in the bush. Signs and wonders.

June 21—I just finished speaking at the women's conference and called Jide. Praise God for the great opening night. Every lady was in the presence of the Lord. Thank you, Jesus!

June 25—Praising God! The conference was glorious! We had asked for His glory, and day after day He came. All the funds needed were more than provided by the Lord—Jehovah Jireh.

July 6—Sensed a breakthrough in the Spirit and heard the good news! *The INS has finally given us our visa renewals!* We praise Jesus for His wonderful ways. *Never give up on God's word!*

July 28–August 4—We have spent the week working exceptionally hard. We thank the Lord for the opportunities. I went to preach twice in San Bernadino with the children.

August 6—Always praising God! Today we received the date for the Women of Destiny 2002. The Lord spoke the word "Independence," July 4–7. Here we come in the name of the Lord!

August 8—I signed the contract with the hotel for the next conference. The deal is definitely the Lord's blessing. We are excited about what we will see Him do in 2002.

August 10—Standing on the promises of God who is faithful. He has told us to fight and be at peace, knowing the victory is already ours in Christ Jesus.

August 17—For the last two weeks I have been receiving a repeated unction to again attend a women's conference in Florida. I've been able to obtain a hotel at a wonderful rate in peak season. That it was available was the hand of the Lord. I had been repeatedly told on at least four previous occasions that there was no availability.

The Lord also gave victory over booking the airplane ticket. After I had received two "not possible" on the required dates, I finally received a yes to travel on the desired day. We know these are the hallmarks of a journey planned by Him! Exciting. Thank you, Lord.

August 30—We received an update from our immigration lawyers. One agency down and one more to go! We praise the Lord for His wonderful works and favor!

September 8—I met up with a Korean lady at the children's elementary school, a Mrs. Kim, who invited me to visit her Korean church. It turned out to be a very large congregation. I attended their English service and had a wonderful time there. Planned a visit for the family next Sunday. Amazing! The Lord had previously spoken to us about people in Asia. We are simply pursuing Him with all of our hearts. His plans, which are marvelous, are ever unfolding.

September 11—The New York tragedy, it's so, so sad. Many lives lost. The nation's spiritual atmosphere has temporarily changed. We are praying for all the grieving families. We will never forget.

September 15—A national day of prayer. People from Jide's office and everywhere went to church, even those who were not Christians. We remain in prayer for the nations.

September 16—We went as a family to visit the Korean church; everyone loved it. Ebun and Remi (acid test) had a great time! We are thankful to the Lord for the reception we received. I signed up for the "How to speak Korean" class. We are just so in awe about how the Lord spoke to us some years before with regard to people in Asia and our fellowship with them. Seeing so many of His words begin to unfold before our eyes is an uncommon blessing!

> Therefore, since we have so great a cloud of witnesses surrounding us, let us also lay aside every encumbrance and the sin which so easily entangles us, and let us run with endurance the race that is set before us, fixing our eyes on Jesus, the author and perfecter of faith, who for the joy set before Him endured the cross, despising the shame, and has sat down at the right hand of the throne of God. (Hebrews 12:1–2, NASB)

After more than a decade of intense wrestling with the INS and other government agencies, we finally received our American citizenship! We did not go back on God's word through the many delays, denials, and even both of my parents' untimely passing. From our new God-given country, the United States of America, we are greatly privileged to continue to share the gospel of our Lord Jesus Christ until He returns or calls us home. Everywhere I go, people tell me how my work has filled them up with hope and light and made them feel the love of our Creator in a powerful sense. As at the time of this update, I have written a second book titled *"Giving God Ultimate Love: Over-the-Top Mega Love."* It received national recognition through the NEW YORK CITY BIG BOOK AWARD® as a 2020 winner in the Spiritual category. I am now blessed with a comfortable life in sunny Southern California with the joys of traveling all over to proclaim God's good news. Seeing my family and loved ones all doing well can only be credited to God's amazing grace. I have given you a small glimpse into some of our daily joys and challenges along the way. Your life journey and call from God may be completely different from mine. It may also be less difficult or more challenging, but never give up on God's revealed promise and word to you. Do not quit! In 2015 I released my fourth gospel album titled after the famous hymn, *"Amazing Grace."* Here's a verse from my version of this well-loved hymn.

Through many dangers toils and snares, I have already come,
It was grace that brought me safe thus far,
And your grace will lead me home.

I hope this memoir encourages you to press into and fulfill God's master plan for your life! Be strengthened by His amazing grace.

Always praising Jesus!
Bukky

OTHER BOOKS BY BUKKY AGBOOLA

Giving God Ultimate Love

All Will Be Well